# Pioneer Tales

# Jane Turner & Bob Jardine

*Pioneer Tales* was carried out as an assignment for Milton Keynes Community Photographic Archive. The aims of the Archive are:

DOCUMENTARY:     to record contemporary life in Milton Keynes, with particular emphasis on the city's social and cultural development.

EDUCATIONAL:     to inform present and future generations about new city life; to reflect changes and progress; and to demonstrate the value of documentary photography in a developing community by organising exhibitions and workshops and by publishing work.

PARTICIPATORY:     to generate material for the Archive by encouraging local photographers to become involved in the project.

The Community Photographic Archive is a Milton Keynes Community Workshop Trust Project.

Financial assistance is acknowledged from the Milton Keynes Foundation.

571

Typeset by Gwen Green, Stantonbury Parish Print

(c) Jane Turner & Bob Jardine, 1985.

Published by the People's Press of Milton Keynes, c/o The Living Archive Project, Stantonbury Campus, Purbeck, Stantonbury, Milton Keynes MK14 6BN.

ISBN  0  904847 16 0

L.28

# Contents

*Tourist's view of Milton Keynes. But behind the earth mounds life goes on in the City of the Future.*

4

# Introduction

Milton Keynes is a new city which, for better or worse, holds the prospect of a new life for thousands of people. Our original idea was a book about the people who designed and built it, the experiences of the 'early settlers' who came here in the seventies, and the efforts of those who, in their own way, are trying to inject life into the city. Some of them are friends of ours, others were enlisted as the book took shape.

The interviews and photographs were made over a two year period. Understandably, during this time changes have occurred. We now have not only a city centre and a railway station but a hospital, too. Also, our ideas about the book altered slightly as we became aware of a common denominator which runs through this collection of personal histories.

All the people interviewed possess some quality or combination of qualities which enable them to cope with major upheavals in their lives. We begin to see them as symbols of a spirit which can only be described as pioneering and which expresses itself as a readiness to accept change, to 'get on and do it'. We wanted to portray as many different aspects of this quality as we could and the final selection was made on that basis.

The majority of interviews take a positive stance towards new city life. This is not due to any desire on our part to present a glowing image of Milton Keynes. Rather, we think it has to do with the fact that the more you put into the place where you live, the more you get out of it.

This book is dedicated to all the pioneers. You've got to believe in the myth if you want to help create the legend.

**Jane Turner**
**Bob Jardine**
*March 1985*

# The Philosopher's Tale

## MANFRED AMBROSIUS

*The soft Irish brogue belies the Teutonic-sounding name. Since moving to Milton Keynes, Fred's philosophical sense of humour has seen him through the breakdown of his marriage and an extended period of unemployment: he is bitter about neither. He doesn't judge people and consequently has friends in many different walks of life. Warm-hearted, gregarious and with many a good story up his sleeve, he believes that life is what you make of it. On a social level, all kinds of opportunities exist in a new city — but you won't find them by staying at home.*

I came down from London six years ago. That was an idea knived up with a friend of mine and his missus and my girlfriend at the time. It was like — we didn't even know anything about the place — just a load of houses. We were living in a one bedroom thing in London — stick your feet out of bed and you're in the oven! So my mate and his woman came down first and then I ended up coming down and staying with them, working here for about three months and then BUMPH! got a house in Stacey Bushes until — how long have I been here? — six months in this flat now.

I did six years in Wolverton Works and I only gave that job up because I broke up with my old lady. That was a strange business really. I packed everything in, you know, when your whole world falls to bits — eight years, nine years with her. I decided that's it, I've had enough, I'm going back to Ireland. So I went back to my old home town. I had to sleep five weeks in a tent so I decided I'm not staying here, I'm going back to Milton Keynes, at least I can get a house back there, or a flat — which I did.

The way they work it is, if you come now there's a waiting list of four years, if you live outside the area that is, for a borough council house or flat. But if you have a marriage break-up it's only a three month waiting list. The best way to get a house in Milton Keynes is to marry somebody with a house, move in with them then get a divorce and go on the three month housing list straight away — you know, citizenship!

Milton Keynes isn't that settled. People keep moving in and out of the city and a lot of couples are breaking up. It seems like a bit of a trend nowadays. I know it happens all over the country but Milton Keynes stands out a bit more. There's people living together for two or three years, and the next thing is a divorce which makes one of the two homeless. They cater for that in Milton Keynes. They figure that if you don't have any rent arrears you've got a good record and aren't a gamble.

Milton Keynes is good. What was it I heard in the pub the other day? Somebody said: "If you can't make it in Milton Keynes you'll never make it in heaven." Why? You've got everything here, it's great! The things I've done since I've been in Milton Keynes — horse riding, lead singer in a rock'n'roll band! Yeah, there's a

## Plenty For Kids

photograph of it in the toilet. That was good fun that was. The band was called Nasty Habit. We got on that local Channel 40 TV doing a live interview. That was a scream, that was really funny. That was about four years ago.

There's plenty for the kids here. If they want to sit in the house all day and do nothing then that's their prerogative. Admittedly it's cold now but there's the old cycle paths, you can go anywhere — Woughton Campus, Stantonbury, Wolverton. As for the evenings, the Chieftains were here a while back, and that play 'Monkey'. Northampton's just up the road. We went to the theatre there the other week, only 70p. It was brilliant. Oxford's not far from here. Admittedly, if you haven't a lot of money it's hard, but I figure everyone's got enough money to do the things they want to do. Even on the social I figure with a couple of quid, like a fiver or a tenner, you can do things. There's the cinema — only two here I know — but Newport's a nice little place. You can go there and there's quite a good pub across the road you can go to afterwards. But if you spend your money on booze you're not gonna have a lot for anything else. And I know for a fact

*Cocktail waiter at Austen's nightclub (formerly The Starting Gate) Central Milton Keynes.*

'cos I suffer from that! I go drinking just about everywhere in MK. I haven't really got a local.

I was staying down in Peartree Bridge for a while and I ended up working behind the bar there. They had rock bands there and the bikers moved down 'cos they closed the back bar at the Starting Gate. Anyway, I got to know the bikers because of that. They're a nice bunch of blokes. Local pubs? I like the old country pubs. New pubs don't have any personality, unless you get a nice crowd of people. But that takes a while and then the breweries seem to change the staff around a lot if they don't like the way a pub's being run. They'll sack the barman and he might be the nicest guy in the world. One barman who was at the Starting Gate — Jim — he's down in Leighton Buzzard now.

## Meccas And The Like

Ever such a nice bloke, but because he'd let the bikers in the brewery got rid of him to get rid of the bikers and then in the end they closed the whole place down. Turned it into a nightclub. What's that gonna be like? Meccas and the like Guys with dicky bows and monkey suits on, throwing their weight around. Bouncers and watered-down drinks at extortionate prices, charge you three quid for the privilege of going in. I don't really like 'em.

Wolverton Works was all right if you had a good job. I started off there crane driving in the lifting shop and ended up there shunting. I loved that, it was great taking coaches in from the main line, bringing them up and distributing them between the various shops for repairs. We were just walking along with them directing the engine. It was a nice feeling 'cos people had to get out of your way otherwise they'd be killed, simple as that really. So not only was there a good amount

of responsibility — nice if you can handle it — but it was pretty dangerous. You had to be fairly good at what you were doing 'cos you could be killed. I nearly had my legs taken off once. I slipped on the ice and my legs went right underneath the coach while it was still moving. The engines weigh seventy-six tons or something like that. You wouldn't have a hell of a chance if one of them crushed you.

That comic I read, you know, 2000AD, they've got Brit City in it and the whole city is run by robots. All the British people do is go to the seaside. They only come up every three months to collect their leisure money. Not dole money or unemployment benefit but leisure money! 2000AD is a big part of my life. I get withdrawal symptoms if I don't get it every Saturday. I've had every one since the first one came out on the 26th February 1977. But I don't have duplicates of the ones I papered on the walls. That was a mistake really. The reason why I did it was, when I moved in I thought to myself I like this place and I don't want to leave and to make sure nobody makes me I'm gonna glue a load of these comics on the walls so if I do have to leave here I'll take this wall with me! Next Saturday it's the three hundredth edition of 2000AD and I'm gonna have a bit of a party to

## The Milton Keynes Mutant Association

celebrate. It'll be the gathering together of the Milton Keynes Mutant Association. There's a satellite in outer space that is like Las Vegas, a big gambling casino. Johnny Alpha and this bunch of guys called the Milton Keynes Mutant Association had collected all this money to go up

and try to win. They did win but on the way back they were mugged. I got the name off that and I thought this is worth celebrating and because it's my birthday I decided to throw it all in together. I wrote a letter to 2000AD telling them about it, so I might get the three pound winner, you never know. I don't really know who'll be coming. All my close friends will be here. They all know I'm nuts about it.

*"If you can't make it in Milton Keynes you'll never make it in heaven."*

9

# The Architect's Tale

## DEREK WALKER

*Derek Walker was chief architect/planner for the Development Corporation from 1970-76. He applied for the job because he felt that Milton Keynes was, at that time, "the most glamorous project in Europe". Now back in his private practice, he lives and works at Great Linford (though he also teaches in America, principally in Los Angeles). One of his current projects is the design for Wonder World, a theme park at Corby.*

Milton Keynes was designated in the late sixties and the master plan approved shortly before I arrived as Chief Architect and Planner in 1970. The pressure on the Development Corporation to get things built after the lengthy planning process and enquiry was intense.

The most telling contribution I made to the New City was the recruitment of a superb professional team of architects, planners, landscape architects, interior designers, technicians, modelmakers and quantity surveyors. The economy was buoyant and consequently we had a multi-national team in the early days, as to many designers Milton Keynes promised to be a world design show case. The climate we created was immensely stimulating and we had tremendous fun. In the early years forty or fifty of us worked sixteen hours a day and the lights of the Development Corporation rarely went off. People were working until eleven at night and would be back again at seven in the morning.

## The First Priority

The process of design and building is a lengthy one and much of the city you see now was conceived in those early years. The first priority was with design policies as opposed to individual schemes — the existing settlements, the villages, the landscape policy, attitudes to parkland systems and infrastructure. The pattern of the city today is about these decisions.

Milton Keynes was going to be the largest, in terms of growth, of any of the New Towns built in the United Kingdom, but there were only about six hundred people in the building trades in the designated area in 1970 and we estimated that the need was 8,000 to meet the original programme. An early problem was convincing contractors that there would be work here for the next twenty years and therefore it was going to be worth their while to move here, but to begin with, most of them would 'bus their workers in from as far away as Stevenage, and that was very costly to contracts not overblest with generous budgets.

At that time we built to a cost yardstick. A specific allocation of money for each public housing unit. That allocation goes down as the density goes down and as our mandate was to build a low density city (we were as one in the condemnation of the still fashionable high rise density solutions for family living) so we bit the bullet and by ingenuity and a little rule bending tried to produce the best possible housing with lower cost allocations. In the early years this meant disappointments — light weight systems and traditional contractors on the same bidding lists, which led to some strange compromises . . . It seems extraordinary to think, looking back, that Netherfield was designed in brick.

Politically there was a swing away from the New Towns Movement in 1973-4 and life got increasingly tough over the next few years. The Labour Government started putting more money into the inner cities and when the Conservatives came to power they backed privatisation as a solution for the New City. This meant little or no more public housing and that is a tragedy for any new town, because good public housing must be the backbone whether built for rent or subsequent purchase. The quality of private housing in the City is a great disappointment to me — it is not of a high enough standard. It is good to mediocre when it should be good to excellent. In space standards, landscape and layout it lags far behind the public housing unless it is in the higher price bracket.

*"It seems extraordinary to think, looking back, that Netherfield was designed in brick."*

We tried to make sure that in a hundred years' time certain characteristics of the city would be memorable. One hopes it is going to be exquisitely landscaped. It will have beautiful parks, it will have a very handsome city centre because the quality of design between the buildings (forget the buildings themselves because they will change over the years) is delightfully urban. The plane trees in the boulevards will be eventually seventy feet high. In twenty years' time the varying quality of individual buildings is going to be less conspicuous because the real quality of the centre is going to be the landscaping and infrastructure which binds it together. The design team worked hard to ensure that the one thing which would always survive in the Centre and Central Area Housing was the quality of the infrastrcture and the space between buildings.

My real frustration is that we have lost a whole series of projects that would have helped mature and beautify the city in a very positive sense. In the city centre we have lost, with the demise of the City Club, the chance to look at leisure in a much more interesting and original way. Discos, a bingo club and a cinema complex is not what I would call leisure for a place like Milton Keynes. For its size there is not enough of regional significance for people to do yet, and despite the Community Workshops, localised activity in the schools and local centres, there is still a massive need for a central centre for arts and leisure activity.

The great problem in England is that leisure is in the hands of unbelievably uncreative and ill-assorted bedfellows, impoverished members of the aristocracy, brewers, ex-professional boxers and bookies, and the new diet for Milton Keynes is far from stimulating as yet The lack of leisure facilities in Milton Keynes has made it something

of a pioneer town. It is those cultural overlays that I feel are essentially missing. An awful lot of people in the community are doing a fabulous job. There is no shortage of characters living in the city but I wish we had a Paul Getty to underwrite galleries and permanent collections . . . The patronage that our Victorian forebears offered their home towns with that mixture of charity and guilty conscience that gave us so many fine churches, museums, galleries, parks and follies, is no longer available. Life and business, alas, is in the hands of accountants and bureaucrats. The sky has become very grey and we tend to get gruel now instead of apple pie.

# The Patina Of Age

Even what we have could be better. I would like to see a much more volatile management in the shopping building and more late night activity areas. I long for the second generation of kooky shops which extend the range of possibilities from a diet of Boots and Woolworths. This is the great problem of City building. Only the patina of age and change brings the balance and variety the population deserves. I suppose one continues to be guilty that with the greatest will in the world a Development Corporation cannot underwrite instant maturity and balanced facilities.

Many of us who worked on Milton Keynes had trained in America as well as England and one of the fashionable academics in the sixties was Mel Webber — he was the patron of personal mobility; the mobility brought about by universal car ownership. The oil crisis in 1973 and the depression of the eighties places that dream into perspective. Though the city was designed to have a comprehensive Red way pedestrian system away from the grid roads, it was recognised even with

our visions of personal mobility that public transportation had to be comprehensive and inexpensive — this to me is an area of primary failure. The electrically operated buses which would have linked Central Area Housing and the City Centre, subsidised by the Centre's profit levels has not happened. Dial-a-Bus withers and dies and the total concept for the City's major bus system is less than adequate for a dispersed city as we now have it. We have got the worst of both worlds now. We have not got the adequate bus service that was envisaged and we certainly have not got the personal mobility because people cannot afford it. Good transport should be a principal priority in any developing city — it cannot be seen as a luxury.

It is difficult to isolate one's most satisfactory collaborations architecturally. It is easier to be more satisfied with overall concepts, but two of my favourites in which I have had a hand were the Sewage Works and the Shopping Building in Central Milton Keynes. The first because it was retrieved from a fate worse than death — scheduled as an engineering nightmare, we made architecture out of its seductive geometry — and the Shopping Centre because it provides the centre of the city with an environmental quality which I hope is contagious.

Of what has been built I think the local centres are not interesting enough or creative enough in small business opportunities. Politically the marriage between Central Government, Local Authority, Development Corporation and County tends, like most committees to water down the gravy. Compromise is not really a word that should describe the design and construction of a new city . . . but in the end that unfortunately is what it is about.

# The Senior Citizens' Tale

## BILL & MOLLY SPOONER

*Bill and Molly 'retired' to Milton Keynes from London when most of the city was still on the drawing board. Instead of putting their feet up, they became involved in voluntary community work on their estate. Twelve years later they're still more active than most people half their age — which just goes to show you're never too old to be a pioneer.*

**Molly**: We came to Milton Keynes in September 1972 and this estate was the first to be built. It borders on to Stony Stratford and we liked it because we were attached to the older part of the area, not like some where they've built houses in the middle of a field. We liked it very much from the word go. We think our flat is ideal for old persons like us. We've got a small garden back and front and there's only two lots of old people in each court — all the other flats are occupied by single people. The young people have adopted us

## Marvellous Neighbours

and we're 'grandparents' to most of the children around here. We've got marvellous neighbours but we didn't realise how wonderful they were until I was taken ill and had to have a pacemaker. Then they came up trumps. Also, when Bill was in hospital they gave me a lift to Northampton every day so he never went without a visitor. They did it out of kindness.

When we came the rest of the city wasn't built. There was just a lot of houses and they all looked alike. If we visited anybody we had to take our boots off on the doorstep or we brought in half the clay of Buckingham! And of course there were no pavements or roads or anything and even the gardens hadn't been laid out then. But the corporation showed us pictures of a wonderful flowering city. We don't know where it was, but they said ours would look like that eventually. But we didn't wait for them to do their stuff. My husband bought turves and laid the lawns. We had a sack of daffodils given us which we planted under the trees — and so we had the first flowers on Galley Hill. Everybody came round to see the first flowers.

We never saw the flat — we took it unseen. We didn't even know where it was. We arrived at the station at Bletchley and no one seemed able to tell us how we were going to get to Wavendon Tower (*headquarters of Milton Keynes Development Corporation*). We couldn't find a taxi — there were no buses outside the station. But finally we found a taxi and the taxi man took us out to Wavendon. It cost us quite a lot and he left us at Wavendon and drove off. So when we'd been interviewed and got our keys and paid our first two months' rent we were stranded at Wavendon. We hadn't seen our flat and didn't even know where Stony Stratford was. Anyway, finally we got another taxi which brought us to the flat and we paid him off. It was quite an expensive operation!

When we'd seen our flat and gone outside, a milkman turned up on the step and said: "Can I be your milkman?" So I said: "I don't see why not. Can you tell us where there's a bus station so we can get a bus back to Bletchley?" He said: "I'll do better than that, if you get on my milk cart I'll run you round to the bus station in Stony." Which he did. So our first day consisted of him running us around to the bus station on his milk wagon so we could get to Bletchley to catch the train back to London. We didn't know there was a station in Wolverton.

I used to work voluntarily on the desk at the Community House. Roger Kitchen and Margaret Lever were the arrivals workers and round them they got a team of us people who'd moved in to help welcome the people as they arrived — most of them from London. Some didn't have any furniture, especially if they'd been in furnished accommodation. I knew a couple with a small baby who'd only got a bed. They'd been allocated a house but they certainly didn't have enough money to furnish it. So we

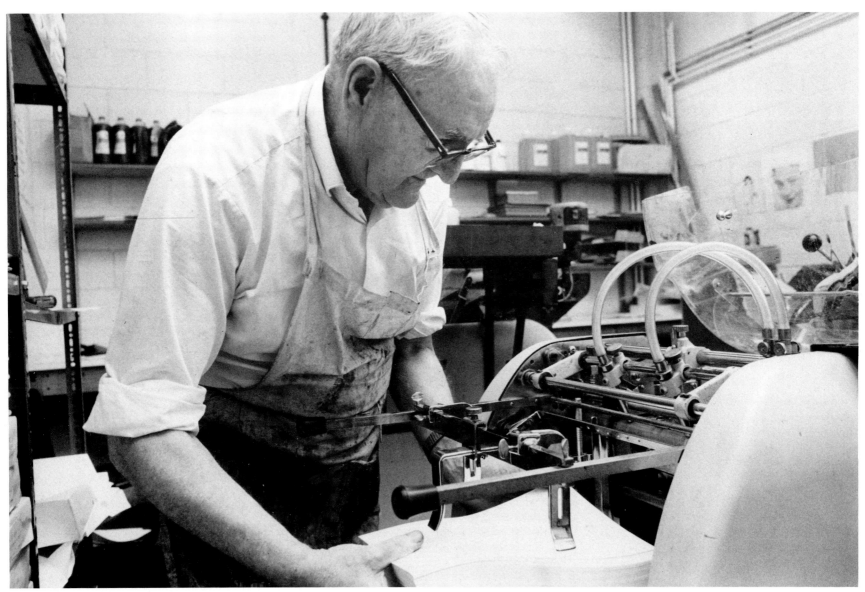

*Bill prints the Galley Hill community newspaper at the Media Centre, Great Linford. The paper is called The Noose — a pun on 'news': Galley Hill used to be Gallows Hill, site of the Stony Stratford gibbet.*

had a scheme going called Tugboat. Some of the families who came up here were a bit more affluent than the rest and they decided as they'd got a new house they were going to get rid of their old furniture. Tugboat would pick it up and store it in MKDC garage that they'd allocated for us. So when people turned up without anything we rallied round the flag boys, and as they became better off themselves they'd sometimes give the furniture back to Tugboat to be reallocated. It was an on-going scheme so people could get a bit of a home round them without going into a lot of HP.

# We Never Considered Ourselves As Old

I didn't have any preconceived ideas about what Milton Keynes was going to look like. They gave us all the paperwork to look at, but I waited to see what the place was going to turn out like. I still think Milton Keynes is a long way from finished because all these fields that we're now looking at, one day — not in my lifetime 'cos I'm too old — but one day they'll join together and then you can call it a city. At the moment it isn't a city, there's no cathedral. It's just a lot of housing estates and one big shopping precinct at the moment. But one day all the fields which separate the estates will be built on because the population will grow.

As for the things we've done, well, we helped to get the old people's club started. My husband's 76 and I'm 72 and we've never joined. We never considered ourselves as old. In the early days of the club we had visions of exercise to music, interesting people coming to speak, but now it's just an afternoon cup of tea and bingo.

So we're not involved with it any more. I helped start the whist drive at the school and now we've got quite a nice whist drive going. The teachers from the school are very helpful and we've got some young people who come and play. Also, we've got a good swimming club. Mothers and babies go on a Thursday afternoon, parents go one evening.

**Bill**: I started up the allotments. There's now a statutory rule that so many allotments should be allocated per housing estate. We started at Greenleys, but it wasn't very successful because it wasn't fenced in and people were getting their vegetables stolen. We also got involved with the community newspaper. I'm now looking at the very first issue, printed in June 1972. It's very interesting looking back because under the heading Postbox it says: "With a bit of luck there will be a permanent postbox on Galley Hill soon. But in the meantime the postman will collect the mail daily from the Community House." But since then, thankfully, they've built a postbox, telephone kiosk and a shop on Galley Hill. In the Community House, where we did our welcoming thing, we put tables and chairs and we used to provide free morning tea or coffee and chats so that young mums who were a long way from London and their mums could get together and make friends. We've always had a good Community Association here. People took advantage of it and it worked beautifully. That is one of the reasons why this estate has been so successful. Everybody knows everybody else. We helped run dances — we had one or two very nice dances and the school allowed us to use their hall.

We helped with a holiday playscheme where volunteers took 20-30 children. The wife and I decided that as I used to be a keen fisherman

we'd take some of them fishing. We found canes and made some fishing nets out of their mums' old stockings and we took 20 children to the river Ouse and a splendid day was had by all. At five o'clock they didn't want to come home. After that, to our surprise, there was a knock on the door and a gentleman stood outside who said: "Are you Bill Spooner?" So I said: "Yes" and he said: "Well, I would like to give you these." He had three bracnd new fishing rods with all the tackle which was a present to the children. We had a competition to win them.

I used to collect old newspapers in my car. Altogether we made £100 which was given to the Community Association. The paper I had left I sold for £9 and we went out and bought some material for a Father Christmas costume. One of the ladies in the court made it up for me, I've been the Father Christmas of Galley Hill ever since. The children see other Father Christmases in the city centre and elsewhere but I'm always their real Father Christmas. Also, on Christmas morning, I go to Newport to The Green, the old people's home, and give out their presents.

**Molly**: He does about seventeen engagements as Father Christmas every year.

# The General Manager's Tale

## FRED LLOYD ROCHE

*Fred was the Development Corporation's chief executive officer for the first ten years, during which time the physical pattern of the city was established. At the time of his appointment he was the youngest general manager of a new town and the first with an architectural background. He left because "it was becoming somewhat bureaucratic towards the end". He is now Deputy Chairman and Managing Director of Conran Roche Ltd., a firm of architects, planners and development consultants based in the city centre.*

I was invited by Lord Campbell, the Chairman of the Development Corporation, to come to Milton Keynes in 1970. We had a series of meetings and I was offered the job of Director of Design and Production. In 1971 the Chief Executive left and the Board asked me to succeed him. I left the Development Corporation in 1980.

The quality of what you build is dictated by economic, social and political considerations — made in central government and at Board level. Designers are often left with the problems after decisions have been made without the full implications having been realised. If you can influence the decision making you can affect policies and resources, which enables you to provide a higher quality of environment.

The way the organisation works is with a non-executive Board of which Lord Campbell was Chairman. The Board decides strategy and policy and those decisions are carried out by the Executive Management Committee. The EMC is comprised of the directors of each activity — architecture, planning, estate management, housing, finance and social development.

Under the New Towns Act, the Corporation is given powers to negotiate for land at certain pre-determined rates and in the last resort it has the power of compulsory purchase. In the event, I don't think compulsory purchase was used at all, the land was all acquired by negotiation, although the powers were always there in the background.

In 1970-73 there was quite a large amount of public capital investment available from central government. With a project as large as Milton Keynes, there will be phases when there will be money shortages and others when there is going to be money available. One key to success is to do as much as possible when and how you can.

In the early years we stretched infrastructure very wide. We built a lot of infrastructure, and when the lean times came, having opened up that land we developed it for a few years until we could get some more money for infrastructure. The whole process has been called one of sophisticated chaos.

## A Thousand Houses Per Annum

In 1971-2 we became successful in attracting industry into the area but because of labour and material shortages we couldn't get the houses built fast enough. We were summoned to the Minister of Housing and told that we would have to provide pre-fabs. We refused to do that and introduced industrialised building instead. If you look at Netherfield, Coffee Hall and Beanhill, they were built at a time when you couldn't get bricks or tiles in the quantity we needed because there was a building boom on at that time. Don't forget we were trying to build a thousand houses per annum and the materials and labour just weren't available. So it was either a matter of saying to firms: "No you can't come", which would have been a tragedy as they are the firms which now form the economic base of the city, of putting up pre-fabs which would have remained permanently, or building those houses.

If you look at the quality of houses from 1975 onwards when the situation became much easier, on the whole we've achieved a quality of housing as good as, if not better than any other community throughout the world in the last thirty years. But them I am a bit biased.

For the first five years — and we always recognised this was going to happen — it was absolute purgatory, because this part of the

country was very rural. This monstrous new city came along, churned up the countryside. There was mud all over the roads and we were never able to achieve perfect phasing with other facilities — public transport, adequate shopping provision and health care. I said sophisticated chaos earlier, and it really was. You have a plan but there are so many external pressures — building strikes, changes in government, cutbacks, changes in health authority, a thousand and one factors. And trying to make all those things work in programming is immensely complex.

The most important factor in the success of Milton Keynes is that in ten years of relative national economic recession thirty thousand jobs have been brought into the city. To create a new urban community with a sound economic base for the future is the major task. One talks about the unemployment levels in Milton Keynes but if you take the number of new people in the city and compare that figure with the number of new jobs and imagine that you could build a brick wall around Milton Keynes, you would see that there is full employment in the city. What's happened is that Milton Keynes has become a regional draw which means that understandably, the unemployed from Dunstable and Leighton Buzzard and the rest of the Region come into the city for work which leaves fewer jobs for the residents of Milton Keynes.

In terms of the original vision a lot has been achieved. Employment continues to grow, the city centre is an immense success. I wish there were more commercial recreation facilities particularly for youngster, but that was a matter of the pressures of the market place which was not ready to provide it.

I have always believed that the quality of environment does affect a community's attitudes and behaviour. If you look at Central Milton Keynes, the quality of the place and its management has meant that there is virtually no vandalism and the degree of vandalism in the city as a whole is very low. I believe a major factor is because the people have responded to the quality of the environment. It's a very high ideal but in trying to provide standards of excellence in all aspects of the city, the hope is that one would affect peoples' attitudes and make the place a more caring one. There are indications of this but it is not as manifest as one would have hoped and is a very elusive quality to define. There are still a lot of old people in the city who feel neglected. There are still deprived kids. So it's not as caring a place as one would have liked to see but I suspect that applies to society as a whole in the seventies and eighties.

18

*"The whole process has been called one of sophisticated chaos."*

# The Doctor's Tale

## Dr. DONALD WRIGHT

*Dr. Wright and his wife live in Homeworld, a development of innovative, experimental houses on Bradwell Common. It was originally built as an architectural exhibition and owning a house there is still "slightly like living in a goldfish bowl".*

*Now chief partner in the practice at Eaglestone Health Centre, Dr. Wright was the new city's first G.P.*

Prior to coming to Milton Keynes in January 1974, I was a practitioner in the southern part of the county where I ran a single-handed practice for nineteen years. For various reasons — personal and professional — I looked around in 1973 for a new job.

Milton Keynes was an unknown quantity at that time. I knew what I was giving up but I had no idea what I was being offered. The brief was that I should start the first of the proposed new

## How To Avoid Mistakes

health centres in Milton Keynes and eventually work with five partners. There were already other practices here, of course, in Newport Pagnell and in other existing communities, but there was no health provision for the new city itself. I knew little about a primary health care team. Luckily, I was sent around the country to visit similar types of health centres to find out what was particularly good or bad about them, and how to avoid mistakes in Milton Keynes.

For the first six weeks of my job I sat on my backside and did nothing. The temporary health centre at Tinkers Bridge, where I was to start work, wasn't finished. It seemed to me that the Health Authority were dragging their heels. I remember one day, there were chaps fitting lavatories at one end of the building and chaps removing them from the other end! After six weeks I got hold of the Health Authority and told them that I intended to start work in a matter of days. If the place wasn't finished in time I would invite the press along. There was feverish activity that week end, and I did indeed start work on the next Monday.

You can imagine that there wasn't much to do at first because we didn't have any patients.

As a doctor you are not allowed to advertise so I couldn't recruit patients. Things gradually built up, however, and my first partner joined me. After a while we had too much work and we took on a doctor from Australia. He had a drug problem, which we knew about and thought we'd try to help him and give him a chance. I'm afraid he only lasted sixty-three days, and went back to Australia. So another doctor joined us instead. Poor chap had a terrible time. Six weeks after he joined us he was involved in a 'cause celebre'. It was all ill-founded and resulted in some very nasty publicity. It was a terrible time. That all happened in 1977. Later that year a fourth partner joined us and things became easier again. We then took on a fifth doctor so we'd never have to rely on a locum.

There was a medical masterplan for Milton Keynes that stated that doctors should involve themselves in community work such as child development work. In the early days I used to go and give chats to the kids in Simpson school, which was great fun. An awful lot was expected of you to make yourself known and to meet other people, priests, school-teachers, architects. With another doctor, I used to do a programme for the community radio station. We had to do it anonymously — we were just "the doctors". We would chat on a certain topic and people would phone in and ask questions. I think it did a lot of good.

The work itself in Milton Keynes is no different from anywhere else, but it often seems that the demands made on us are higher. In general, the sort of problems that are presented here are the same problems that appear in Birmingham or Bermondsey, but they are perhaps highlighted here because people have been uprooted. We are all immigrants here. I'm very enthusiastic about Milton Keynes. It's the only

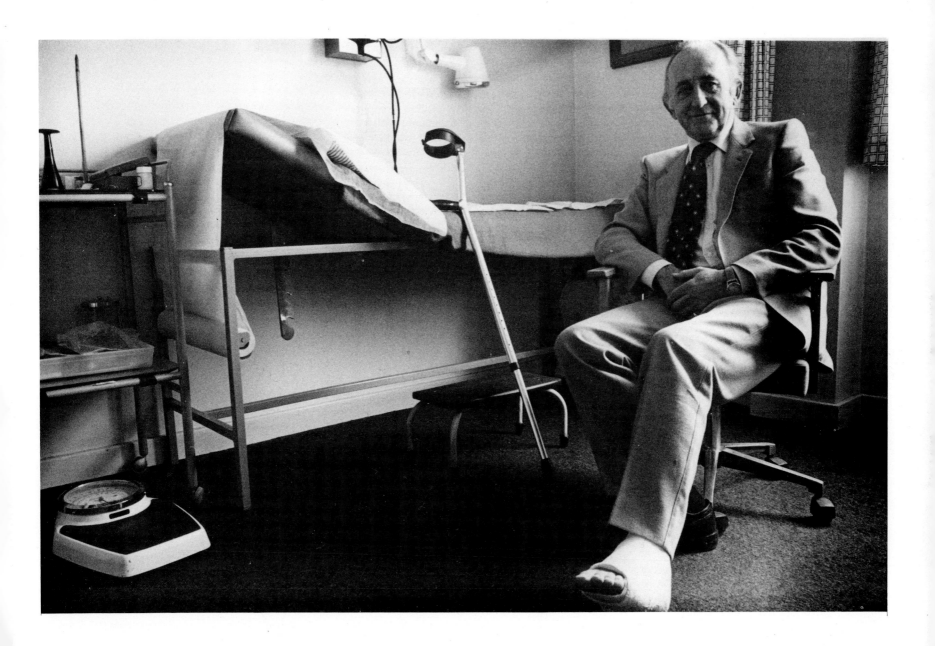

21

place in the world where you can say it is better this week than it was last week because there's always an improvement. For a time, I think the city went to sleep and we all lost a bit of impetus, but we were given a big lift when the Shopping Centre opened. I think the same was true when the railway station was built.

There is a tremendous number of young people here and therefore I see a lot of children, due to understandably-anxious mothers who feel a bit lost not having Mum and Granny living up the road. They lean fairly heavily on the health visitors, the social workers and their doctor because they need someone to relate to.

The object of having a health centre is to get people to come to the doctor rather than have so many home visits. In general we try to arrange that people can have an appointment of six or seven minutes. That may not seem much, but your problem, or the problem of the person before you, might only last a minute. Someone has wax in their ears, one sends them off to see the nurse who will syringe them. So the next person has seven minutes plus six due for the person before. Or, if I think you have such a problem that we're not going to be able to do it justice I'll suggest that you come back another day and ask for two or three consecutive appointment times. Then I don't feel rushed and nor do you. I never know how long I'll spend with a patient and I don't look at my watch.

I get to work about ten past eight every morning although I don't start seeing patients until nine; there's always letters to read or dictate. Then I will see people from, say, nine to eleven o'clock, then there will be business to attend to. We always arrange that there will be one doctor here all day, so that if people ring up there is a doctor they can speak to. The public could help us enormously by reducing their demands a little bit because some of the problems that come our way are not really ones for a doctor. I think if people knew that the chap who works from eight in the morning until six at night is also the bloke that's on duty at night they'd be rather more sympathetic to us. A lot of the people in Milton Keynes come from big cities where they have deputising services and the doctors only work from nine to five.

There are various clinics going on all the time, for instance ante-natal clinics and cervical smear clinics. We started doing cancer smears in 1974 and some of our work in that field has achieved some recognition. I appeared on Anglia Television last year in a ten or fifteen-minute programme in which I was interviewed. During the first clinic we ran we had found a lady of sixty-four who had cervical cancer and she's still alive, fit and well ten years later. She also appeared on this television programme. She was chuffed to bits and said: "If I hadn't come to see the doctor in 1974 I'd be dead now".

# The Teacher's Tale

## PAUL FREEDLAND

*Paul and his wife Chris were among the 'early settlers'. Both active Christians, their decision to come to Milton Keynes was based on the belief that God was leading them. In those days the Promised Land was just that: a lot of land and a lot of promises for a city of the future. Paul recognises, however, that his 'way' isn't necessarily the way society is heading. We each have our own path to tread — and we must find it for ourselves. It isn't something which can be taught in school.*

We're both Londoners, born and bred in North London. I was in my probationary year teaching not far from where we lived. One of the leading lights in the Parent Teachers Association was doing some work in Milton Keynes, his company was building some houses. He got to talking to me about it. I'd heard of Milton Keynes but I hadn't thought anything about it. This was eleven years ago, the place hardly existed then. Anyway, we started thinking about it and as Christians praying about it and we decided to move. On the face of it, it was a good time, the kids were young and the prospect of getting decent housing in London was virtually non-existent. So I suppose housing had a lot to do with it. I didn't have a job lined up but I'd always had a fairly strong belief in my abilities as a teacher, so I felt that wouldn't be a problem, particularly in an expanding situation. Dedicated teachers in the primary sector tend to get on fairly fast anyway.

I contacted the Education Office here and said that I was interested in working in Milton Keynes. There weren't any jobs at the time but they said they'd let me know. I kept phoning them and in the end — largely to get rid of me, I think — they sent me to see Kit Welchman who at that time was running Simpson Village School. He was recruiting staff for a new school at Simpson and I said that I'd be very interested. I spent a day there and fell in love with the school and with what he was trying to do, and with him as a person, really. He's always been a kind of mentor for me. I was offered a job as a scale one teacher when I'd finished my probationary year.

There was no house available so I stayed with friends during the week and went home to London at weekends. After a whole term and a considerable amount of hassle we got a house and moved into Tinkers Bridge. We were the first ever people to live there. Shortly after that we had a severe gale which blew down some of the houses which were under construction, and so for the

## Our Own Community House

next four months there was only us and about four or five other families living on the estate. But we had our own community worker and our own Community House and an arrivals worker and everything — but no one else, because they were worried about the strength of the houses. There was a lot of hysteria at the time. It didn't really bother us — we were very much in the process of just loving all the freedom. In London we'd lived on the first floor of a house, in a non-selfcontained flat, with an old lady downstairs, and we had three children under the age of five. Everytime Chris wanted to go out she had to bump the pram down the stairs and then get the kids to the park because there was nowhere else for them to play. Just having our own front door was fantastic.

It's difficult to imagine now because Milton Keynes is such a civilised place, but in those days it was primitive. Shopping was Bletchley, and not even Sainsbury's existed then, you had to go to Northampton or Bedford. During that time it was very much like being a pioneer. Netherfield wasn't built, and apart from Tinkers Bridge there was nothing else in the South of the city at all. The only other estates that were built at that time were Fullers Slade and Galley Hill in the North, which were miles away. The city centre was still being farmed.

I stayed at Simpson for five years, until I moved to Springfield School — where I became

deputy head and eventually headmaster. I believe that schools should be essentially human institutions, and that the accent should be on 'human', rather than 'institution'. It's inevitable that a state school is going to be a bit institutional — your customers are there because they have to be, not necessarily because they want to, and on the whole they are only at a particular school by the accident of where they happen to live.

I believe that a good education doesn't parcel people up into little packages of 'social', 'personal' and 'academic', but takes the person as a whole and tries to develop that person as a whole human being. Social education, in terms of helping kids to understand where their place is in society, is as important as anything they might learn from a textbook or from the blackboard. A school is, in fact, a community in microcosm and one of the most important things we can help children come to terms with is how they relate to different people — their class teacher, their peer group, people they perceive to be their enemies, dinner ladies, school secretaries, welfare assistants, visitors, people we meet when we go on school trips. All that is about learning to deal with life. I've never believed that school is a preparation for life, school is life. The kids are people and they are members of a community *now*. If you are going to set up an institution that has a human face, then the notion of enjoyment is an important one. So we try to make our curriculum lively and adventurous, we try to take the kids out a lot, we bring in visiting speakers, so it's not the same old boring stuff from books, the same teacher teaching the same things, and so on. The relationship between the class teacher and his or her pupils should be more akin to that of a friend than somebody who is held in fear and awe. The fun side is very important.

The whole of our school code of conduct is based on the idea that we want everybody within the school to behave for the benefit of the whole, and that the benefit of the individual is secondary to that. But that is a message that is doomed to failure because there is so much pressure outside of school — from the home, from the television, from society as a whole — which generates the notion that the most important person in life is oneself and after that you might care to think about other people. The more you can acquire and the better you can do for yourself the better everything will be. That is not something which I feel is a satisfactory philosophy for life.

# I'm A Workaholic

I enjoy working to the point where I probably drive people to distraction. If Chris was here she'd tell you that it took her a number of years to convince me that holidays were a good idea at all. I'm a workaholic, really. I don't enjoy sitting down and doing nothing. I don't like watching telly all that much, although if I'm tired I might watch something mindless on the box. I'm devoted to my job. I love it, so to work is to play, really.

Christ is very much the centre of our lives and the church is an important part of it. We're members of Coffee Hall Community Church. For the last two or three years I've been an elder or leader. Most of the time I've run the Sunday School, although for the last year or so Chris has been doing that. I lead services and do a bit of visiting and the things that leaders in churches do.

I would hope that my Christian belief and commitment goes with me into school and my attitude to headship is one of servanthood, a sort of servant/leader figure, not an autocrat. I would expect to do my share of the grotty jobs, washing up, sweeping and clearing up and all the nitty-gritty things that have to be done because I think it's important that leaders do that. Christ himself sets us that example. Hopefully my attitude towards parents, to kids and to my colleagues is all coloured by my Christian conviction. But when it comes to the teaching of religion, then I don't believe that I have any mandate whatsoever to use my position to evangelise. So my assemblies are absolutely non-religious. We never pray and very rarely sing anything that could be called a religious song. I don't think it's right that state schools should be in the business of proseletising or propagandizing for a particular religious point of view. I think it's right that children should be taught *about* religion, but true religion, in my opinion, is a personal experience and you can't teach that. You can only preach that and encourage people to join you in it, and that is not the role of a school teacher. I think that one reason why the church has such a bad reputation nowadays is the R.E. that kids learn in school. I think it would be a positive thing for the church if it were banished from the school curriculum.

I don't see myself being head teacher of a primary school for the rest of my working life. From the professional point of view, I honestly have no idea what I'm likely to do next. It will depend on where we feel God is leading us.

# The Executive's Tale

## JERRY LATHAM

*Commerce is the economic lifeblood of the city. During the seventies a number of large companies moved to Milton Keynes, providing employment. Today we take their existence for granted. However, the task of moving a major national company to a new city is fraught with all kinds of hazards, social as well as economic. It involves risks which must be faced with confidence and commitment.*

*When VAG UK Ltd, the British-owned distributor of Audi and Volkswagen cars and parts, decided to centralise its operation Jerry Latham was the Project Manager in charge of the company's relocation and development in Milton Keynes. Unlike many senior executives he made a personal commitment as well as a professional one: he chose to live within the city boundary.*

In the early seventies we became increasingly aware of the need to centralise and operate the company from a single location. The first consideration, obviously, was to decide where to go. As one of the principal benefits was going to be cost saving in the distribution of parts our choice was reasonably limited: we couldn't go to the north of Scotland, however low the development costs of a warehouse might be there, or to the southwest tip of England or to one of the east coast ports. By examining our dealer network and our distribution pattern we arrived at a map of the country indicating the most logical triangle in which we should be based to get the maximum benefits out of centralised distribution. We defined the triangle as an area bounded by Swindon in the west, Northampton to the north and Watford to the south. Research indicated conclusively that we should base out main operation somewhere within that triangle. We needed good road distribution throughout the country, we needed an airport not very far away and we needed access to rail transport. We also needed to be sure that there would be an adequate supply of labour with manual, clerical, secretarial, managerial and specialist skills, to cover the varying needs of our different operations. These include warehousing, data processing, accounting, and administrative functions as well as the many specialist and technical activities of our industry. We also believed there had to be an attractive living environment because we were aware that we had a large number of 'key personnel' who we wanted to bring with us.

Between late 1975 and the end of 1976 we looked at probably in excess of eighty sites within our triangle. We looked at 'spec' built warehouses and offices but in the end we decided we wanted to build our own. Milton Keynes Development Corporation responded very positively. They showed us sites, they showed us what they were doing, they talked about their plans, they showed us schools and housing. It was apparent to us that they had as much concern as we did for the environment that would be provided for people who came to live and work in Milton Keynes.

## An Attractive Proposition

To us, Milton Keynes was ideally located. We found a site of the right size with enough room for expansion. The deal was realistic. They didn't give us the land or do us any particular favours in the commercial sense. But where they really impressed us was the back-up service they provided in terms of visiting our existing locations and talking with our staff about housing and schools, and indeed any other specific or personal subjects that concerned individuals. They were very much on the same wavelength as us. We didn't find that attitude anywhere else within our triangle.

We, on the other hand, were an attractive proposition to the Development Corporation because we were one of the first major employers to move here. We were going to provide over six hundred jobs in the city. I think that we were the style of employer that they wanted, a company that would want to get involved in the area. Also, we were bringing our head office here, not just our warehouse. All new cities run the risk of becoming warehouse cities because companies put up large distribution and storage centres where relatively low numbers of people are employed. We were bringing not only a quantity of jobs but a variety — management, secretarial, technical, catering staff, a complete spectrum. At that stage in its development there was no doubt that it was important for the city to attract big names in

*"To us, Milton Keynes was ideally located . . ."*

companies.

I'd been involved in the original discussions, but was due to go and work abroad in another division of our parent company. I was about to leave when it was decided to commit the necessary capital to moving to Milton Keynes. It was a project which particularly interested me and I decided to stay on the basis that I would be involved in the project. I ran it from its conception to completion and for a year afterwards because there was still a lot to be sorted out after the move. It was a tremendously interesting job. Now, I look after our dealer network development.

I spent a lot of time looking at Milton Keynes as it was then. I had to come to conclusions about whether I believed what were very ambitious plans. At the time, a lot of people viewed some of the things the Development Corporation were saying with a degree of cynicism. There weren't many companies here. It was one huge building site, a lot of mud on the roads, the trees really were little in those days. To a certain extent I shared this cynicism, which I thought was healthy. I went into it in a lot of detail and from the views I gathered at that stage I came to the conclusion that if I was going to be in the persuasion business — persuading the company that they'd made the right decision, persuading the employees that it was a good place to come to — it would look a bit funny if I was living twenty miles outside the city. So from one point of view I felt I ought to live in Milton Keynes. Having said that, I don't think I would have come if I hadn't wanted to. From what I found out I wanted to be part of it. I found Milton Keynes an exciting concept and I saw the opportunities for getting involved in its development. The city was at the beginning of its life and I loved everything I saw. It pains me immensely to hear the joking references to Milton Keynes

made by people who've never been here and don't know anything about the place. Of course mistakes have been made. It wouldn't be what it is if somebody hadn't had the guts to let people do different things, and in the end you say: "Okay, that was a mistake." But I think many of the mistakes are now being put right, some of the early housing estates, for example. I think it would be unreasonable to expect that people who live here won't find anything wrong with it. But there's much more that's right, and good, and worth being proud of.

# We Were Overwhelmed

As the first step towards moving the company we took a temporary office — The Mount in Simpson — for a year. We had our project office there and moved a personnel team in. Towards the end of 1977 we put a single advert in the Gazette saying we were moving to Milton Keynes the next year; we would be looking for staff and we'd like anyone interested in working with us to contact us. We invited them to come to an open evening. By six o'clock there was a queue half a mile long. Over six hundred people came to see us that evening and in the end we couldn't physically see them all. We had to print forms on the spot and ask them to fill them in. We were overwhelmed but enormously encouraged, too. The quality of people applying was far higher than we could have anticipated. You used the phrase 'pioneering people' earlier and I think that the very fact that they'd moved to Milton Keynes said something about them. They were people who wanted to become involved, wanted to get stuck in. They weren't just looking for a nine to five job, they wanted to be part of something. So, as we became clearer about which specific jobs

needed filling we called on that initial pool of people. Today several years on, we remain well satisfied with that aspect of moving here.

We started construction on site in the spring of 1977 and opened our warehouse in May 1978. The logistics of transferring from six locations around the country, moving people, stock and equipment here was a period of maximum risk to us. Our whole parts distribution system would have broken down if we'd got it wrong. In August 1978, over a single Bank Holiday weekend, we moved the whole company here. In retrospect it was a dream project. It was enormous fun as well. We've been here for just over six years. There's no question that we are a better company, a happier company, a more efficient company. There is more of a family and team spirit now we're all on one site. No regrets, no looking back; we're all part of Milton Keynes today.

# The Film Maker's Tale

## DUSTY RHODES

*Dusty's tale is one of extremes of fortune. Coming to Milton Keynes gave him the opportunity to realise a "burning ambition" to work freelance in film and video. He's taken several gambles along the way, usually for all-or-nothing stakes. At one point he lost everything he possessed.*

I used to visit Bletchley — when I was in the Territorial Army of all things — in about 1969. It seems ages ago, I doubt if they'd even accept me now. There was a lot of talk about the new city so I decided to move here. At the same time I decided to train as a teacher because I couldn't think of anything else to do. I got on quite well with kids and was helping out at Derwent Drive youth club. Years ago, Derwent Drive was the one and only place to go and see bands. Status Quo, AC/DC — I could reel off a whole list of people who played there when they were nothing. Anyway, that was why I came really and I decided I'd take a teaching training course and a Youth and Community work course here. While all this was happening I was making 8mm films. I've always been absolutely mad about film. I got my first camera when I was about fifteen. I used it so much that it wore out.

I went to Canada in 1973. I decided with a friend to do the trip all young men must do and we hitch hiked from one end of the country to the other. When I came back I started to get stuck into video. I was working at Derwent Drive again and I was shown some half inch video gear they'd got at the Media Centre. The equipment was a community resource but there were only a couple of groups using it then so I decided to have a go. Unfortunately, one of my failings is that I never like doing anything in a small way so I embarked on this massive documentary drama based on a book called 'The Gates' — the kids chose it — which is all about school-phobia. It was a bit of a mishmash but it was partly about a load of people getting together and making something to put on video. I remember spending hours and hours editing the thing with a stopwatch and chinagraph pencil. Ten years on the equipment is unbelievable compared with what we used then.

If we got it right we were lucky. It was shown mainly to other youth groups but its premiere was at the teachers training college. It was a terrific fascination at the time, everybody wanted to be in it.

## A Real Riot

I was still at teachers' training college and had settled down to the idea that I was going to be a Drama or an English teacher but because of all the video and film projects I was involved with I met this chap called Michael Barrett. He'd been given a brief by the Home Office and the Development Corporation to set up a community cable television station. It would be in programme form dealing with local issues and happenings. He had a look at the things I'd been doing and about six months later turned up at my house one evening and asked if I'd like a job. I said: "Yes!" I jumped at the chance because for me it was the kind of thing that only dreams are made of. I had to take the decision of coming off this teacher training course and take up a two year contract with Channel 40.

Channel 40 was a breakthrough for local broadcasting in this country, although it's been happening in America for a long time. We were one of several projects but the first to be government funded. We did all kinds of things, election specials where we'd courier video tapes about on motorbikes so we could go out almost live. We did a rock show once from a youth club which was a real riot. I spent nearly three years at Channel 40 but at that point there were a few rows. It's a bit vague in my mind now, but I decided to quit along with some other people. Eventually the television station closed down and the whole thing turned into a radio station. The greatest thing Channel 40

gave me was an ACTT broadcast ticket.

When I left I spent all the money I had buying a film camera and all the ancillary equipment to go with it. It was the standard equipment used for doing documentary or T.V. news work. I bought it without having any work and phoned up BBC news. They gave us some film to make a little report to see if we were any good and we took it to a carnival where a local stuntman was going to drive a car over all these other cars. It was quite a good stunt so we shot the film and interviewed the guy and then took the stuff down to the BBC dubbing theatre in London. The guy who gave us the film watched what we'd done, scratched his chin and said: "Fine, great, a few problems with the exposure . . ." But he thought it was good and he said he'd call us and to our surprise he did, three days later. We had to go and sit outside this judge's house and wait for him to come out. He never appeared but we got paid £75 so I didn't mind. The second call was when Lady Spencer Churchill died and donated her eyes to somebody or other and we had to go and see the surgeon. That was the first of ours that was ever transmitted.

Unfortunately, although the money started coming in we weren't getting enough work to sustain us. The car kept breaking down and all sorts of things started going wrong. The last major job I was called out for was for CBS in London. CBS told me to go to Marwell Park Zoo and cover a giraffe called Victor who was on his last legs. I can't remember quite why it was so newsworthy now. Anyway, we arrived late. Just as we got to this bloody zoo the giraffe died and we had to deal with this very irate American female reporter. We got in terrible trouble and I knew that I needed a decent car and a decent camera which I couldn't afford so there wasn't much point in going on. I sold my equipment and got out altogether. In fact,

I set up a furniture business.

It took three years to get the furniture business going, dealing in antiques and stripped pine furniture and that was really hard work. We started off in a kitchen and ended up with God knows how many square feet of warehouse, two shops — one in Central Milton Keynes and one in Olney — a workshop, a London supplier and a French shipper. We went bust in the end. It's easy to forget but at that time, in 1978-79, this country moved into the grip of a real depression. For me, in a business like that, the recession was really heavy. People stopped spending money altogether. Luxury goods plummetted and the firm had to liquidate. Running that company was just plain hard work for absolutely no real returns so I'm bloody glad it went the way it did, otherwise I'd still be working thirteen hours a day and earning less than the till girls in Woolworths.

I dropped out for a couple of years after the firm went bust. I was mentally exhausted and had a little bit of a nervous breakdown. I didn't know where I was going. I just used to sit at home. It's hard to explain, but when you've had liquidation followed by bankruptcy and the people have come and taken all your bloody furniture and every scrap of money . . . All my possessions went. I sat there on my floorboards and wondered what the hell I was bothering for. I've always described myself as a doer but this time it got me into trouble and I had to accept the responsibility for having got that company off the ground and providing nine people's wage packets. After that experience I got ill. Slowly I started reading film books again. I watched T.V. and got interested in watching movies. I got a burning ambition. If somebody had come to see me and said: "If I take those two fingers off your hand, you can direct 'Battle for the Falklands' for

MGM," I would've said: "Cut 'em off now." Because that's what I wanted to do. I started operating cameras again and got back into video. I did a couple of promos for local bands and slowly began getting my contacts together. I invited myself to see people at Sony and had a look at the new cameras they'd got. Then I met someone from Volkswagen/Audi. They'd started using freelance people so I filmed cars and things for them and at the same time got my own projects together again — shooting little dramas because the equipment was available to me. Latterly I've got involved with Videovision Associates. We do music promos for broadcast television and things for pretty big companies, adverts, all sorts of stuff.

It might seem more obvious for me to move to London now things are going well. I can stay with my brother in Hampstead if I need to but there's something about Milton Keynes . . . I travel about the country a lot and Milton Keynes is the only place I know that has this electric atmosphere of let's BUILD, let's DO. And while there's a lot of apathy — quite understandably from unemployed people, and I know what it's like after the collapse of my business — it's in sharp contrast to the other people you meet in Milton Keynes who are generating a hell of a lot of enthusiasm. Very often it comes from creative people who love what they do — fashion designers, artists, people who plug away on their own. Milton Keynes is a tremendous backdrop because of the building and construction and the newness which I think goes hand in hand with creativity. I'm lucky to live where I do. I've got a nice house with the City Centre right outside my window. I was a country boy and I've had the sheep and the cows and the farm and what I love now is right outside — a huge expanse of glass.

# The Reporter's Tale

**SHEILA MACDONALD**

*Embarking on a new career in a field as competitive as journalism takes a lot of guts. Sheila was twenty-seven when she started working for the Milton Keynes Gazette — quite a bit older than most cub reporters.*

*"In this job there's no point in being a shrinking violet because you'll just shrink away and nobody will notice you. We're all quite egotistical, you've got to be to do this job. You need the self-confidence to be able to knock on the door of a complete stranger and say: 'Hi, it's me. Tell me about your most intimate personal life'."*

My parents moved down to Leighton Buzzard fourteen years ago. I was in secretarial college in Scotland at the time, so I stayed behind to finish that and then moved down to be with them. They started running a boarding house there and I started commuting to London to work as a secretary. I was about seventeen then. I did that for a couple of years and then I actually got a job on the building site of Bletchley Leisure Centre as a secretary. That was quite good. I used to do daft things like, I'd get really bored and put on a donkey jacket and go down on the building site. I'd help them count how many doors had arrived for the stockman or order lorry loads of gravel and grit and things. And if it rained you had to go to the postbox in your wellies and donkey jacket so that was good fun. I didn't actually ever see the Leisure Centre completed because I decided to go to university then. I went to study at Birmingham doing social sciences for four years. I majored in psychology. Meanwhile, during those four years my parents moved to New Bradwell and the new city was starting to get built. I used to come back on holidays and get on buses that were going the wrong way and there were no signposts and I used to hate the place. I had four sisters that had all moved into the area, but not having a car and not being a driver I had to rely on buses and, as I say, Milton Keynes was just being built and you always seemed to get dumped in the middle of nowhere.

I went abroad for three years after I finished university, got married, came back again and by that time Milton Keynes had really grown and I could find my way on the buses and the question mark that was supposed to be a hospital by then was going to be a real hospital. So what did I do then? . . . I hung about for a bit, my parents had moved to Stantonbury by this time.

I was over in Germany for five months and that's when I decided I wanted to be a journalist. So I came back and worked as a temp. during the day with a firm on Blakelands and did my freelance journalism as well for about a year. The first time I saw my name attached to a story I rushed home and pasted it in a scrap book and thought of the sixteen thousand people who'd read it and then after a while you think yeh, but none of them will remember my name or what's been written.

## A Story To Me

There were some silly things happening in Milton Keynes then that obviously hit your eye as something that people would want to know about like, I'd be sitting working away in Blakelands, miles from any water and this lorry would drive past with a barge on it heading off for the motorway. I thought, my God, what's a barge doing up here? — It just happened to be a firm that did the old traditional designs on the barges and they hadn't been able to get a site on water so they had to work away from water. So, that was a story I did and I did one about Stantonbury Campus because at that time it was very forward looking in comparison to a lot of the older more established schools and they were introducing more equality into the curriculum and that appeared to be a story to me. And then we had the Buddhist colony down at Willen Lake and one of the nuns there, Nara, is an English girl which I thought was unusual. I did something on that and 'She' magazine bought it from me. So I thought, right, this is it, I'm on my way. Luckily a job came up with the Gazette so I applied for and got it and I've been here ever since.

The first horrible story you get to do once you start taking on some responsibility, is

*Buddhist monks shopping, Central Milton Keynes.*

going along to interview the family of someone who's either committed suicide or died in a car accident or something like that. It really hit me in the gut. Suddenly it's not all nicey-nicey reporting, it's doing things you don't want to do so that you can communicate to other people. The first death story I remember — I don't know if it's the first one I ever did, but it was the first one I really felt sick about — was when a bloke had hung himself in his back shed on Heelands. I went along to interview the family and . . . I don't know, you seem to switch onto a purely informational level. You turn off any emotions. Your job is to go in there, to get the facts and to try not to upset anybody too much. You have to feel that you're doing them a service if all their neighbours can read the paper it means the family won't have to do so much explaining. With a bit of luck they're not going to meet somebody in the street who asks about the health of the deceased. You knock on the door and say: "I'm terribly sorry to bother you. I'm from the Milton Keynes Gazette. I've come to talk with you about the terrible tragedy . . ." and all the rest of it. You know then if they're glad to share the burden with another person or resent the intrusion. They'll invite you in and then it's a question of going through the facts with them. "Oh, who found your husband? Where was he?"

"He was actually hanging from a rope in the shed." You're watching yourself and thinking, "Oh, my God, how can I do this? How can I ask these questions?" I did all this, got my facts and figures, enough to write the story and I drove the car away round the bend and I couldn't drive any further. I had to sit there for a while. I was shaking and felt sick at myself for what I was doing and felt sick for these poor people. Nobody knew he was going to kill himself. I don't think I'll ever

get hardened to it. But reporters are a bit like undertakers, we've got a wicked sense of humour. We make jokes about people who have died and the way it happened between ourselves. You do get a bit cynical but when you're actually meeting the people who it has happened to I think you'd have to have been born a pretty hard person not to let it get to you. It does always touch you. Having said that, relatives often like to talk about it because by the time you see them they've already spent three days with relatives who are sick to death of hearing how miserable they are, or, they feel themselves: "Oh, God, I mustn't keep going on about it. It's very nice of my sister to come and look after the kids. I must try and appear calm." So the reporter is another ear for them to tell things to, and with a bit of luck they're not going to meet somebody on the street who says: "I haven't seen your Ian for a while, how is he?" That's part of local reporting. It's not nice to do, but you can see it's worthwhile.

# Heart-Warming Stories

There are some heart-warming stories too — elderly people who get married. I must admit that we tend to groan at the thought of doing another golden wedding. They always say the same thing. You say to them: "You've obviously managed to survive marriage for fifty years and that's quite a thing these days. How have you managed it?" And they always say without exception: "Oh, we've had our ups and downs. We've had our good times and our bad." And you think you'll go mad if anyone else says that. I like the really daft stories like the practical jokers who bought their Italian friend a donkey for his birthday because they always said that Italians weren't fit to be driving cars. I went along

to do this story about this poor guy. He didn't know what to do. It was in his back garden and he thought he had it for life.

I must admit I enjoy living in Milton Keynes and through my job I've met loads of nice people. Most places I go I can usually see someone who I've met before so it makes a very varied social life for me. But career-wise there isn't another move I can make here unless I go into radio because there isn't an evening paper in Milton Keynes. The only way to stay here would be to commute to London and work in Fleet Street or on a magazine, or to work on the evening paper in Northampton. Part of me says, I really like living here, I've got most of the things I need. I've got a nice house and a garden and friends, a lot of good friends, is it worth moving for my career? A lot of people hate it here but I think Milton Keynes is what you make it and to me, a place might have lots of discos but you don't get to know people in discos, you can't possibly because they can't hear a bloody word you're saying. It's nicer to have good pubs and places where there is live music and we've got that. Many people don't look for what's good in Milton Keynes. So much money gets poured into projects in this place and three people turn up and there's another thirty of forty people who'd really have enjoyed it if they'd made the effort. I'm not keen to move but in the end my career is important to me. I wouldn't call myself a ball-chopping career woman but eventually I may well move away. I'd like a job on an evening paper as the next step and then . . . I don't know, see what comes up. I quite fancy a column of my own. I've got quite an enormous ego and I'd like to sound off and pontificate in a Fleet Street paper about things I didn't or did like.

# The Universal Man's Tale

## BILL BILLINGS

*Bill is a hard one to categorise. He's a very creative person, his talents embrace sculpture, poetry, music, painting and invention. During the renaissance the Italians had a name for such Leonardo-types: universal man.*

*Listening to him talk is like meeting an express train head-on with one arm tied behind your back. He can carry you away with the force of his argument, his energy, his anger. His perceptions have been honed by years of struggling against the system. The phrase 'a prophet without honour in his own country' might have been coined for him.*

Who am I? Born London 1938, (but I lie to young dolly birds) hung around Mummy's apron through the war. Daddy was away for six years. Wasn't evacuated — Mummy didn't know how to read the paperwork. We hid under the bed while the bombs were flattening the city. This is all genuine — at the time it was really frightening. There were no bananas on the streets. Never seen chewing gum, fruit, cows, grass. Terrifying experience. Went to the local school three years too late. We didn't have any schools they'd all been flattened. (Hitler had done a reasonable job.) Won two scholarships — one for St. Martin's College of Art — but couldn't go because Daddy didn't have fifty pounds a year. Went to Highbury Grammar School. Believe it or not Rhodes Boyson — now Education Minister — was headmaster, but he didn't teach me to speak 'properly'.

## Soldier Called Up

Was a teddy boy, six button jackets but I looked better in four, (that's a lie, I never looked good in any of them, but I thought I did.) Wasn't a bad dancer — (laughs) — I did win a Butlin's competition once. What a prick I must have looked. Never had your oats until you married. Youngsters wouldn't understand that. Soldier, called up. Arrived at the army camp in my teddy boy gear. Sergeant-major hated the look of me with my sideboards and my pearl button waistcoat. Decided to destroy me, chopped all my hair off . . . Soldiers, Signals, found out I was intelligent, made me an instructor, eighteen and a half years old, Corporal Billings, Royal Signals, 23440278, stamp it on the brain and on your heart in case you ever got killed they'd open it up and there it is printed on the heart, Billings for the use of, article 1, expendable persons. Did a few courses. Went out to join the Arab army. Don't ask me any more about that — I was frightened and got a few medals.

Came home, marriage went on the rocks, crawled into an attic, met someone who says can we get a proper house without being married — and we ended up in Milton Keynes in a council house and I remembered that when I was fourteen I won an arts scholarship to St. Martin's. I wondered looking out of my sludgy heap on Netherfield what I could re-capture. I went out and built a concrete sculpture for twelve pounds of my own money for my daughter. Lord Campbell comes and gives me a pat on the back. Then I do a beach-buggy, then a tree-house, then a giraffe and I teach a lot of people to do a lot of things but I find that I can't get aboard the gravy-train.

I'm on the dole then, doing part-time bits and pieces, jobs, prisoner, ain't got enough money to get out, trapped.

I built three concrete dinosaurs but only one has survived because I didn't belong to anybody. I didn't work in an office, I was just somebody living on Netherfield doing it, who hadn't actually consulted anybody. I wanted to put one in Linford Wood but they wouldn't let me. But if you go to Crystal Palace you'll see dinosaurs. I've seen things like that all my life. It's nothing risky, they're successful. I knew it would be successful before I did it. My dinosaur is the best selling post card they've ever done. They never asked me — they've made a fortune out of it, never given me anything for it, ever, not a penny.

I built the first dinosaur on Netherfield. I scrounged the materials and built it in the middle of a field. A brontosaurus, and they just destroyed it. I thought they had a point there, they said it was dangerous to children, they'd fall off it and it was near the road. So I went a built the second

one, a stegasaurus, down at Bleak Hall which was in the middle of nowhere. They destroyed that one too. Same old story really, I hadn't asked anybody. Well, after that I really got my anger up. I thought that's it, I can't accept that. I'd come to this new city where everybody's supposed to have a chance and I thought well, that's no chance, so I'm going to show you people how to have a chance. The only chance you get is fight. So the third one, the Triceratops at Peartree Bridge — which is the one on the postcard — I had to sleep in it for three weeks while I was building it. There was a petition to knock it down from Eaglestone residents. They said it devalued their property.

I wrote poetry then about the whole situation I've been talking about. It was published in 1977. All right, the world don't owe you a living, but I felt I'd put so many years work in. I thought at least something would have come out of it. I'm not asking for money, I was asking for . . . I suppose it's recognition, that's the word really. The poetry was successful because I went to London. It wasn't through Milton Keynes. I went to London and because I was from Milton Keynes and spoke about something that was 'out there' I was successful. People were interested and I went over to America and read at Harvard. So Milton Keynes isn't the only place that's got these weaknesses I'm talking about. I've done four books and had my poetry translated into Finnish, French and German.

Looking back, I think I had novelty value because I was rebellious. It wasn't because of my talent, they didn't care about the content. I was just a guy who was against the system which hurt me really. "Lorry Driver Writes poetry." I got the same pattern of events with the T.V. people. You get on National T.V. but you're only

valuable when you're serving them. They're going to do another programme next week and the week after, but you're finished. The cameraman works fifty-two weeks a year and so does the assistant and the researcher . . . you don't, you're gone. So any young artist who thinks: "I've made it, I've been on T.V." — that's it. The depression sets in when they all go away and you realise you are in exactly the same position as you were before. What you need is a poxy wage and a salary. What you need is patronage, and patronage doesn't come from Jim Bloggs down the road, who's on the dole, it comes from THEM. The patronage has to be not an itchy little fee, goodbye, how clever you are, what a wonderful job but we're off to the South of France on a three month sabbatical. I don't want to be poor. I'm fed up with being poor, I've been poor since 1938. It's a stigma. It's like being on railways lines. The system says you can be anything you want. You can't, you can only be a product of the social background you come from.

I'm now employed by the Borough Council doing arts and crafts projects with local kids. They gave me a nissen hut at Stantonbury which I turned into a children's workshop. It was very successful. We had a play scheme in the mornings with over thirty children attending. In the back we had a children's workshop and we did all the props for the last two Milton Keynes Festivals in the playground, and we also had bands practising two nights a week. It all went well for two and a half years and then some idiot came along and burnt it down which really took the wind out of my sails. If things like that happen you do get edgy. The more you do the more enemies you make. I did everything with a good heart and I felt I had a note in me that the city needed. Everything I've done has been successful. The murals that I did three or four years ago in

Bletchley are untouched, that's true. Now I have this room in Alex Campbell school which I use as a studio and the kids can come and paint. But if everything had gone according to plan I'd be part of a team, using my skills and contacts to make a practical injection into the city. They say they've got these people but I don't think there's anyone as good as me. The job of a community artist is to stimulate and give people confidence in their own ability — you know, the joy of life, making art live and be practical. I don't want to define it I'd rather do it.

A lot of the strength in my character is due to the twelve years that I spent in the army. I learnt how to wash my socks and iron my shirt and make my bed, although I did miss Mummy for the first six months and when I went on active service I did cry and suck my thumb. The discipline and training I had stood me in good stead for all the rebuffs of the artist in society, in MK particularly. You have to do it on your own. You can't even look to the working class people around you for help, because they partly don't understand what you're doing until you've done it. All you get from the working class ranks is: "He ain't that clever else he wouldn't keep doing it amongst us." And you go to the bureaucrats and they say: "Well, if you're that good you'd be like one of us." D'you get it? You have no safety. You have to believe in your own talents and feel confident.

Do I think I've made it? Yes, because I didn't do it for financial gain alone. I made it as a person. I've been vulnerable and said how I felt. People can take me out of context and use it against me, but it's been happiness not unhappiness. Maybe the unhappiness I've had to absorb within me. But you go and ask the kids, hundreds of them. They respect me. Funny, but I've never felt that respect from the people who are paid to respect me.

# The Vicar's Tale

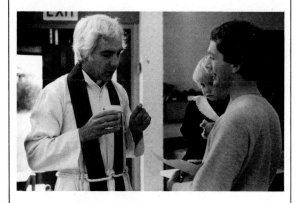

## REV. PETER GREEN

*Peter was ordained into the Church because of "a gut feeling that this is the way I've got to live my life". Born in east London, he came to Milton Keynes after working in Sri Lanka and Sheffield. He is married with three children and lives on Downs Barn. With Gwen, his wife, he also runs a parish press which is based in their house. The print shop is in the kitchen; their bedroom houses typesetting equipment. In addition to his duties as vicar, Peter, like many of his colleagues these days, is deeply involved in community work, and in particular the Community Workshops.*

I am part of the clergy team for the Stantonbury area, which is all of the grid squares north of the city centre. My first job was to see whether a Christian community could be developed there. There was already a tiny group of about five or six people who were meeting before I arrived. They had been found by members of the Christ Church congregation and they included a number of people from Conniburrow and Downs Barn. We used to meet on Sunday mornings for worship. We met together, we prayed together, we attempted to sing — appallingly badly — and it started from there. We decided we'd meet once during the week as well for a time of thinking and studying, to see what happened. We originally met in the Small Meeting Place on Downs Barn and we gradually outgrew that and moved across to the school. It's difficult to say why people become part of the growing Christian community, but they do, slowly.

## Paid To Live Here

I see my role here as being very much the same as in any community. I think that the old title "parson" is quite a good word. One is a "persona", the person who is around. I'm the only person on this estate who is actually paid to live here and to be here. When people say: "I know you're busy Peter, but . . ." I say: "Look, I'm paid not to be busy. I'm paid to have the time." It doesn't always work out like that. One gets caught up in lots of things which may or may not be important, but theoretically I'm the person who is *there*. If it's two o'clock in the morning and there's no one else you can think of you ought to think: "Well, there's someone who's paid to be available and that's the vicar." So one gets a certain amount of counselling work but not all that much. One doesn't try to do the work of Marriage Guidance. Obviously they are very busy so you do pick up a little bit but it's not my specific skill. There's a certain amount of dealing with people who are disturbed or upset, and of course people who are bereaved or who are planning a marriage or baptism. And I suppose the "hatchings, matchings and dispatchings" part of the job does occupy quite a lot of time. In a sense I find that the most interesting part of the job because one is dealing with non-church people. Church is always, in a sense, family. Non-church is outside the family and there are advantages in getting outside the family from time to time.

The parish press is not really my job, my wife runs that. We started a community newspaper way back in 1973 and because we needed to print it we bought an offset litho machine. It's located in the kitchen of our house. You can do almost anything you like in a vicarage, and certainly you can print church material. Whether we print other things as well is of course another matter! Gwen takes the beginning of an income from the press and we do a very large amount of church work, not just local but national as well.

Part of my job brief was not only to build up a community of people — who are the *real* church — but to see whether it was appropriate to erect a building for the church. In conjunction with the residents' association on Downs Barn, we decided on a building that wasn't just a church but a community centre and meeting place for the estate as well. We shall probably start building in 1985 on a site at the junction of Downs Barn Boulevard and Over Street. It'll be a church, community centre, vicarage and a block of six small commercial units. We shall probably rent one of these units as a print shop. We didn't ask the architect to make it look like a church. We asked for a building that would do certain things, that would be a church, a playgroup, a coffee bar and

*"I could get a licence for the school but I don't think anyone would want to get married there."*

which would have an outside yard for the children to play in. We did say that we wanted at least one room that would be the chapel or quiet area — the shrine, if you like.

# Unity Is Not An Easy Option

The church in Milton Keynes, like anywhere else, is complex. The mainstream English churches, namely the Church of England, Methodist, Baptist and United Reformed Church, all work together throughout the city as one ecumenical church. The Roman Catholics and the Salvation Army work independently, plus there's a cluster of independent churches like the Conniburrow Free Church and the Netherfield Congregation, and there are the fringe sects which may or may not want to claim the label of being Christian. So I'm part of the mainstream English tradition and as far as we're concerned we're a group of four churches working together to serve this part of the city, twenty grid squares in all. It's much more difficult for these churches to group together in older, established areas. It is a trend that is welcomed by many of us, but there are some people who vociferously oppose it. Unity is not an easy option anywhere.

The Church of England policy is to have someone working in each area, rather than have a big church with a large number of staff — which goes back to what I was saying about the role of the parson. The image is *leaven*, hidden away, rather than having an enormous cathedral on the top of a hill. Each congregation is different. The new converts in our own community are all under forty. This year we presented five adults for membership and the average age was thirty or

thirty-two. These are people who have had no previous Christian experience at all and who have been prompted, presumably by God, to become part of the life and work of the church. They just turn up on Sunday and say: "I think God wants me to come to church." Then they take part in a time of preparation and are eventually accepted as members. Within every Christian group there are three categories of people. Those who are strong, confident, mature and able to sustain themselves in the knocks and hurly-burly of life, they are the workhorses. There's another group of people who have been injured in life, either mentally or physically, and most good congregations have some workhorses and some members who really need care and help to get them over their difficulties. And thirdly there are those who enjoy coming and for whom worship is valuable, but who don't contribute obviously to the life and work of the church. Who can evaluate their hidden contribution? They are part of us.

Each denomination has its own law which is a mixture of English law and church law, and as far as the Church of England is concerned only certain buildings are licensed for marriages. I could get a licence for the school but I haven't bothered because I don't think anyone would want to get married there. So if someone asks me to preside over their marriage then I'll borrow another church, usually St. Andrew's at Great Linford. Similarly for funerals. Baptisms are slightly different, they don't need a building. They are not a legal thing at all, they are a statement of faith and can take place anywhere. All you need is some water and we use a cut glass bowl. Unfortunately we broke it recently. We're using a Pyrex one at the moment!

I'm not the sort of person who carries a future pre-packaged. I came here with a reasonably

open mind. I'm an optimist. I assume everything will be all right. In my job it's important to listen and think and I don't really know where the institutional church is going. Many of the things the church used to do have been taken over by the state. The church's job is to come up with new ideas about what's necessary. I really hope that the community church we are building will be able to be the centre of community life, as if the community was an extended family. One of the things that is difficult about Milton Keynes is that people haven't got grandma and grandpa around the corner and perhaps what the church has to provide is a network of families which provide that relationship for each other. The other work we have to do is the worship of God and the establishment of justice in our lives, and as Milton Keynes develops we will have more work for the Kingdom of God, to make this new city a Jerusalem, a City of Peace.

# The Community Artist's Tale

**LESLEY BONNER**

*The relationship between artist and patron can be tricky at the best of times. When the patron/employer is a large corporation the possibility of misunderstanding is multiplied: creator and administrator frequently have different terms of reference.*

*However, as a community artist, Lesley has left her mark on Milton Keynes in the form of murals, concrete play sculptures and woodcarvings. Working with local residents including children, her "gallery" has been the playgrounds, pavements and underpasses of the city.*

I came to Milton Keynes after I left art college in 1977. My sister already lived here and I came to stay one weekend at the end of September as I was feeling a bit depressed as I couldn't find a job. She was working, so I went off for bike rides, one of which took me to Wolverton Job Centre. It was purely by chance I went to the lady on the desk and she told me about this job creation scheme that was on at Stacey Hill Studios assisting Liz Leyh, the Artist in Residence at that time. I filled in the forms and got the job. It was supposed to be for a school leaver so the money was dreadful but I was happy because I'd got a job.

Liz was doing various town-art projects, things that she'd make with her team and then put into situ — like the concrete cows — and she was doing the odd school project and a few community art type things. I was one of a team of four on this Job Creation project, three of us had been to Art School so she had quite an accomplished bunch I suppose.

My interest in community art stemmed from a dissatisfaction with the type of art we were encouraged to produce at college — a beautiful finished piece of painting or sculpture, purely for a gallery-going public. I felt this had little relevance to me and became more interested in how art could relate to everyday people. These ideas were all fairly theoretical at College but through getting that job in Milton Keynes I became involved in a practical way.

Liz's contract with the Development Corporation ended in August 1978 and when I joined the November before, the concrete cows were already on the go. Really, they were her parting gift to the city. I don't think they were designed to bring world renown to Milton Keynes. I think she did them as a bit of a joke and because once cows grazed on the fields that the city was being built on. I can't remember the exact reasons, it was a long time ago. Concrete is actually used a lot because it's cheap, versatile, quick and very durable and you can paint it bright colours. You couldn't do bronze play-sculptures.

## The Blooming Cows

Liz packed her bags and winged her way back to America, and practically the same night some person knocked the cows' heads off with a sledgehammer. Meanwhile I'd put an application in to the Corporation to see if I could be funded for a year to do community arts projects because I'd done one or two when I was working for Liz. Anyway, as a result of the blooming cows being vandalised I got a letter from the Corporation asking me to put in a quote for replacing the cows' heads. I did this and thought great, a bit of extra cash. Now, when they sussed that I was the same person who'd just applied for a year's funding they immediately arranged that my first project should be mending the cows' heads. What that's got to do with community art I shall never know. And from then on every time something terrible happened to the cows I was always commandeered to maintain them. Once it was three times a year which irritated me as I was only maintaining my own work once a year or less and the Corporation never bothered to tell me if something dreadful happened to my sculptures. If the cows had a spot of damage I had to drop everything and go and sort it out!

By and large my work was given very little publicity by the Corporation. I made them for and with the local communities anyway so it didn't really matter. I did have one thing publicised by the corporation and I was very cross about it at the time. I did a mural at Great Linford local

*Lesley's griffin at Eaglestone.*

centre and it took six months to prepare with the children from the Gatehouse School for the Deaf. We did an enormous amount of preparation and design work while waiting for better weather and me and Bill Billings and the children spent months painting it. At the same time the Daily Mirror was running a National mural awards scheme. I thought, great, this could be good for the school and good for me so I sent in photographs and documentation. We didn't expect to win but we got a commendation which was quite good. The Corporation publicity machine found out about this and got hold of the BBC2 news programme that has subtitles for the deaf. It was all quite appropriate. I found out through the grapevine that this T.V. crew was coming and it was only by a stroke of luck that I happened to be at the school on that day and I happened to look out of the window. I saw all the cameramen etc. trooping about and I wondered why they hadn't asked me any questions and suddenly I saw this women from the Development Corporation publicity office telling them all about the mural, not letting them anywhere near me. I thought it was a cheek but typical. It was great for the school as it was shown twice on BBC2, but it was the way the Corporation took the publicity of the mural over without consulting me that was annoying.

There are community artists in other towns all doing diverse things, but Milton Keynes begs landmarks and that's what I set out to make. I never did as much as I'd have liked as I was plodding along on my own. The Corporation never had enough money to employ anyone to work with me. As it was, my contract had to be renewed every year until last year when my job finished. I thought the reason was that they'd had me for five years and felt they'd like to fund other community artists but I haven't seen any new blood as yet.

I think all the projects I did were worthwhile. Each one was tailored to the needs of the people involved and the situation. All the things I did were in response to either a request by the local community or by landscape architects to enhance their play areas. And the local community always participated to a large extent, apart from the griffin because the play area was long overdue to be built and I had to make the griffin off site with the help of Community Service Order people and Youth Training Scheme people. But when it went on site I was very conscious that the local people might not want this huge thing dumped in their play area so I got the local school children to design the colour scheme and help paint it. When I was standing outside shivering in the middle of winter I used to wonder about how worthwhile it all was!

# Always Very Careful

When I was working with all the kinds on the wood carvings I was always very careful because some of the kids would be only ten or eleven and I did realise that I had a potentially lethal situation. I used to show them exactly how to use the tools and drilled into them that their feet wouldn't touch the ground if there was any larking about! I must have had lots of kids working on woodcarvings over the years and never had any accidents. In the Oliver Wells woodcarving project we worked one to one with the kids. I had another girl helping me and the kids took turns. The staff and we were very keen that they should all have a go and there were only two who couldn't manage. I had a haemophiliac and a boy with brittle bones working on the carving and they never came to any harm.

I think there should be a place for all sorts of art from gallery art to community art, but my one objection to the prestigious art objects in Milton Keynes like the Figure of Eight and the Circle of Light is the amount of money those things cost especially when that money could have kept me in business for another few years! What really gets me is the amount of publicity these pieces of civic sculpture get and the lack of publicity that's been given to community art projects.

# I Like My Little House

I now work part-time under Manpower Services Commission in a drop in resource centre for the unemployed, catering particularly for people with learning difficulties so now I find I do very little art instruction and most of my time is spent teaching maths and English. It's a job. These days you can count yourself lucky if you have one. I think I'd quite happily leave Milton Keynes if I was offered something good though the idea of packing everything up fills me with horror. I like my little house and garden in Neath Hill; and would be loathe to give it up, especially, because if I was to go to say, London, I'd be back in bed-sit land like I was ten years ago.

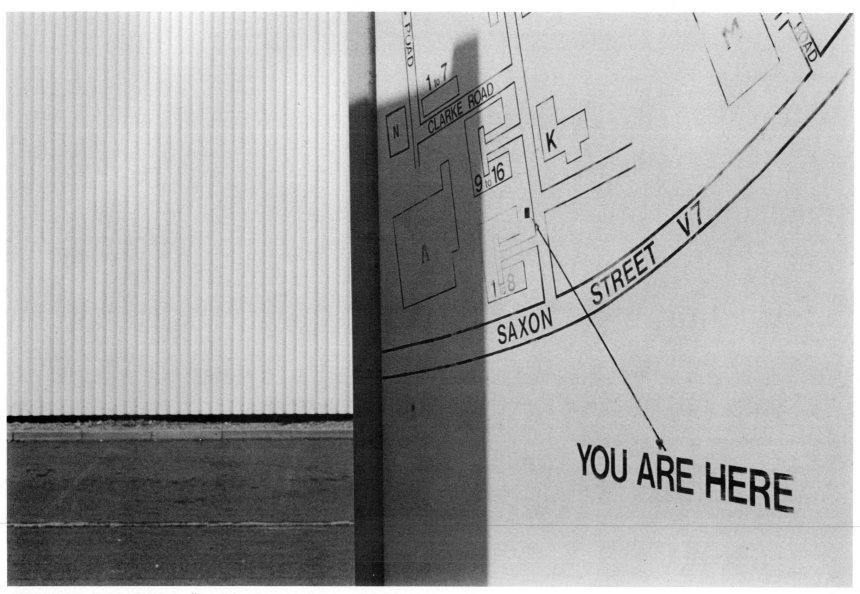

*"Milton Keynes begs landmarks . . ."*

45

# The Ringmaster's Tale

## TOD CODY

*The surname Cody is synonymous with showmanship. Tod's roots are in the circus and in the course of his career as a stuntman and escapologist he has broken every bone in his body. He still performs, but increasingly his talents as an organiser are in demand by T.V./film companies and advertising agencies. Much of his work now takes him abroad. For several years, however, he was responsible for staging some of the city's more spectacular entertainments.*

A popular misconception is that I am a descendant of Buffalo Bill Cody. I am a relation of S.F. Cody, a colourful Wild West character who also ran his own Wild West shows. He had the misfortune of growing a goatie beard, having long hair and he used to like to wear his working buckskins. Little did he know that a few thousand miles away making a big name for himself in penny dreadfuls, was Buffalo Bill Cody, who coincidently had long hair, a goatie beard and buckskins. The two of them became confused and S.F. was known as the imposter.

## A Walking Goatie Beard

We've always been pretty much in this area. The Wild West shows came over in the days of Victoria. Prince Albert himself took part in Wild West shows. There are Codys in Germany and Spain all connected with the circus in some form of outdoor entertainment. So I'm not exactly the last living example of a walking goatie beard and buckskin.

We moved to Great Linford in 1959 from Silverstone by the race track. We had a farm where we used to breed our animals and train them. My father decided that it would be good to have a business at the winter quarters so when we were away money was still coming in. We chose this place because it was a cafe and petrol station. It was going cheap so we bought it cash and moved there straight away but we didn't tell anybody. There was only about one caravan here because we were on tour and nobody knew that come September a small army of vehicles would descend on the village. The council got wind that a circus was coming to town and put a big padlock on the gates. My father said that it didn't make sense as we owned the premises. So obviously we cut the

chain and went in. Police came and served all kinds of notices on us. They hadn't seen a circus in these parts — let alone had one living on their doorstep. They were a bit concerned about the noise from the animals, the trumpets of elephants and growls of lions and other unknown creatures secreted away in 'beast-boxes' as they were known. "Are these animals safe?" they asked, and we said: "No, they're very dangerous wild animals." "And what will happen if they escape?" "Well, people will be injured." I suppose we scared them a bit. Anyway we were forced by a court order to leave our own premises. My father couldn't understand it and got quite upset. He was quite a character himself and we moved our circus into Newport Pagnell and parked up in the Market Square which meant the market couldn't operate because of the various animals — and the trumpets of elephants and the growls of tigers. We stayed there about a week and the police couldn't move us. All the animals were roaming around and we told the law that if they were causing an obstruction they'd better arrest the offending animals. They decided to let us go back to Great Linford until the thing went to court.

Of course we had mishaps. lions escaping and we once lost a bear for three days in the sand-pits. We all went out with torches at night and chairs and nets in the day and the locals would ask what we were doing. We'd say that we'd just lost a dog. "What does it look like?" they'd enquire, but we didn't dare tell them and cause panic in the streets.

It must have been about 1970 when the Linford Village Church Hall Committee were thinking of raising funds for the local church tower and I went to a couple of meetings and we decided to put on a Linford Show. We made it a sort of steam rally with circus-style entertainment

*The Great Milton Keynes Balloon Race (specially staged for the TV advert).*

and pitching bales — all very villagey type things. We made lots of cream teas and a good time was had by all. It was very successful in terms of atmosphere and I think people were pleasantly surprised because it was a little bit different having the circus thing included. It was a good format that continued there for perhaps three years. At that time the Corporation was steaming ahead with their plans and asked if we'd be prepared to move the show into the new city. We were offered a site at Mount Farm by the industrial estate and I was happy to go ahead. I was encouraged to make it bigger by underwriting the event against loss. It soon became more of a carnival and less of a village show. It looked like it should become a bit more commercialised. We couldn't go on doing cream teas, we had to have hot-dogs and ice-cream vans and sponsors. The show moved to Milton Keynes Bowl and I was employed as an entertainments consultant to organise and promote events there for the first three years of its operation — to put it on the map as far as family entertainment was concerned. A lot of people felt the Bowl was purely a pop concert venue. A note of alarm went up, millions of pop fans would descend on MK, and would camp on people's doorsteps, set communes up in gardens. People were worried about their milk bottles, others imagined that their daughters would get raped. So the coming of the County Fair — the glorified version of the Linford Show — helped to arrest these fears. The Bowl was to be seen as a family entertainment venue as well. The County Fair went a long way to provide fun and games for Milton Keynes.

Circuses are successful in certain towns and a rule that I don't know has ever been broken is that if a town is good for the circus, it always has been and always will be good. 'Newport Pagnell' was a term used by circus people to mean death as far as circus was concerned. The people there just didn't want to know. Milton Keynes is not much better. It isn't exactly the entertainment centre of the county and I hate to say it but it's due to the people. It's not just the new city but a kind of apathy in the whole area. However, the opposite would be the Rhondda Valley. You could make a small fortune, even if you went there every two months because the people are circus-minded. The trick is that if circus does well somewhere then any other form of entertainment stands a very good chance. The circus attracts a complete cross-section and is a marvellous gauge. Using this guide we felt that Milton Keynes people wanted more fun and games. They didn't want to sit and watch a four hour theatre performance, or horses jumping for trophies, or steam engine rallies. They wanted to see a bit of everything. They wanted to sample things that they hadn't seen and wouldn't forget

## Glossy Brochures

for a while. People came to the city being promised lots of things by the Corporation and by the media. Lots of glossy brochures, shopping as it should be, every kind of Utopian facility was being offered. Of course they were here and did exist, but you need to use them. Folk didn't get out much if there was nothing on at the cinema and they couldn't get a baby-sitter. So we felt that at least once a year people could get over to the Bowl and dress up and put a funny nose on. Bring your baby along and we'll tell you if it's pretty or not. If you've got knobbly knees you might win a fiver, all kinds of fun and games. We'll do such things as mud-wrestling, we'll try man-powered flight contests and if you want to feel like a bird for 1.5 seconds then fine. We'll let you conduct the Woburn Sands Band, or compete in a pantomime horse race. We were always trying to come up with new ideas and involve everybody, all the stall-holders would dress up and we'd involve the army careers whether they were part of the arena show or not. We'd borrow their jeeps and do some car-jousting. And they all mucked in. But fun and games ceases to be so when you have to become commercialised. I think the County Fairs were designed to last only a few years. In the early stages we brought along things to Milton Keynes that had not been seen anywhere. In those days it was very rare to find a local show that had sky-divers. Unheard of that a flying trapeze act should be presented out of doors — or a high wire act, or stilt-walkers and jugglers and fire-eaters and clowns. After three sky-divers we tried fifteen. Then we dressed them as gorillas. We introduced the world's first female escapologist, anything that was different — mediaeval jousting, chariot racing, car stunts. Sure, things went wrong sometimes but that's half-expected and planned for.

I never came to Milton Keynes to use it as a venue for a theatrical event, it is my home and it just so happened that I worked on my own doorstep for a while. That's not always easy as sometimes it can decry the things you're doing. It's far more glamorous to be able to say: "We're a high wire act from London." People always want to book acts from away. MK is known as an experimental city and if you've got a new idea it is very good to come from here. They assume you've had a lot of backing with which to organise it. MK flies the flag abroad. Certainly when we mention Milton Keynes people are very interested and think of it as a new and exciting venture.

# The Musician's Tale

**JEFF DONERT (KINGSIZE KEEN)**

*Milton Keynes is still a wilderness as far as entertainment is concerned. Mostly, it's down to the efforts of a few dedicated individuals who care enough to want to do something about it.*

*Over the years, Jeff has made numerous attempts to organise concerts and regular venues. But one of the symptoms of new town blues is apathy — and Jeff keeps coming up against it. No one could blame him if he decided to call it a day. So far, he hasn't.*

I've had the nick-name 'Kingsize Keen' since I was in the army in 1960: Kingsize because I used to weigh eighteen stone and the 'Keen' because I'm a musical nut.

I went to Malaya for three years with the army. I arrived at this brand new Commonwealth Camp and got together with some of the lads. We formed a band called 'Kingsize Keen and the Blue Stars' because there was no entertainment there. We performed all over the place and as long as we kept the sergeants' mess happy once a month and played for them for nothing it was OK. They took their ten per cent. We were one of the first bands in Malaya to have Vox amplifiers, the same as the Beatles and everybody were using over here.

I was professional from '66 right through to 1970. I had four years on the road. I started off doing Rock 'n Roll but it was suggested by my agent that if I switched the rock 'n roll pianist for an organist and started playing soul he could get the work backing the American soul artists when they came over. So that's what I did. The first guy I backed was Percy Sledge, the guy who did 'When a man loves a woman'. I backed all the big names, The Drifters, the Ronettes, Clarence Frogman Henry who did 'I wonder why I love you, but I do'. I couldn't get to the top rung, I was always one below. I had a good band but I just couldn't get there. So that was it. I moved back to Southport, my home town, couldn't find a job for a while and almost became a recluse so far as music was concerned.

I worked for National Car Parks in Southport for about four and a half years as a manager. I won the car park competitions every year. You wouldn't find a dog-end on my car park. I had registered disabled staff working for me and they worked twice as hard as anyone

else to prove a point. The money wasn't brilliant and I got about as far as I could there so I became a bit discontented. There was this guy, a season ticket holder and a mate of mine who told me he was off to live in Milton Keynes. So I said 'I'll tell you what, Harry, if you hear of any jobs down there let me know'. Two weeks later I got a phone call off him about a job as car park superintendent at the city centre. The wages and conditions sounded great so I wrote away and got an interview. I fell in love with the city centre as it reminded me of places I'd visited in America and I was determined to get the job.

## A Load Of Flannel

Pauline came to visit me. She heard all the promises, so that was it. I got the job and we moved down. And it was the biggest disaster of my life, because it was all a load of flannel.

I worked here, walking round on foot, running eight thousand parking spaces on my own for eighteen months before they gave me a van and it was twenty months before they gave me anyone to help. In fact it went from the sublime to the ridiculous. They came up with the bright idea of using wheel clamps on cars that were wrongly parked and gave me six staff to put the scheme into operation. For the first few weeks we were clamping twenty cars a day and the drivers had to pay a five pound fine to get it removed. Gradually as time went on it got down to about two cars a week. The word was out. All my lads were dressed in green uniforms and the CB sign for them was the 'green meanies'.

Then the cutbacks came. A year ago last November, I went to the States for a holiday, came back twelve days before Christmas and the

*"Doing the markets is hard work but I enjoy it — and I'm not on the dole."*

Corporation told me my job would be finished on July 1st. It was a big come down. To have been promised all these things and for them just to disregard the whole business.

If you walk round the city centre now, it's chaos. There aren't any height barriers up and I signed for thirty four of them. They're in a store in Norfolk House and people are too bloody lazy to put them up. I used to do an inspection every month to see how many litter bins were hanging off the lamposts. They get smashed in because the brilliant architect who designed this stupid city centre decided to make it different from every-where else by not having any kerbs, so people pull into the parking bays, don't know the length of their car because they're lousy drivers and go smack into the litter bins on the lampost because there isn't a kerb to stop them. It costs forty pounds to replace a bin and every month I used to put a requisite for forty or fifty bins to replace the smashed one. Since I've left, bins have just been left to hang off the lamposts. It's all changed. Cars park on the grass verges or on the disabled bays. Nobody gives a damn.

Once I knew I was being made redundant I wrote off for forty-two jobs. I only got three replies, one was for an interview but I didn't get the job. I didn't know what the hell I was going to do and I ended up in the catering business, running a mobile burger van. The caravan I've got was parked for months behind the civic offices getting vandalised and dirty so I found the guy who owned it and made him a bid for it, did it up and decided I'd go out doing catering on the markets.

I regret ever having come to Milton Keynes but I've really tried to make the best of it. After I'd been here five months and was missing Southport like mad, Pauline said, 'Why don't you get a band together?' Where upon I nearly had a heart attack! She's the first woman I've ever met who's given me any encouragement in that direction. I said 'Are you serious? D'you realise what you've said? It'll take up a lot of time you know'. I advertised for musicians and 'Kingsize Keen and his Rockin' machine' was born about three months later. We often used to play at Muzaks which was a great music club at the New Inn in New Bradwell. When it closed down I really missed it so I went to see the people who were previously involved with the running of it and started it up again.

# And Boy Did It Rain

This town is 'el Floppo'. Have you heard about my flops? Well, Muzaks flopped but it wasn't my fault. It was really sad. The local National Front mob obliterated New Bradwell and Wolverton one Friday night. It was in the papers the following Thursday and after that the attendances at Muzaks fell dramatically. The last night cost me sixty quid out of my pocket because I had to pay the band and nobody came.

Two weeks later I held the Charity Music Day at The Groveway Stadium. I had two stages, seven bands and in all the years I've been associated with anything to do with music I've never put so much into one particular project as this. It was to raise money for four local charities and lots of people worked their guts out to make it a success. And boy, did it rain! There was a gale blowing and I can remember people up on the stage scaffolding holding plastic sheeting over the speakers to try to keep them dry. We had to switch off the juice because the bands were too frightened to play. They thought they'd die. Having said that, it didn't start raining until an hour after it started

so there should have been more people there than there were. It's back to the old apathy of Milton Keynes people who scream that there's nothing to do and usually they're right. But even when people like myself pull their guts out to put something on they still don't come and support it.

I must be mad, but I'm trying again. I want to get Milton Keynes people interested in music. I found this great pub in Southend where it's all happening, loads of bands playing, musicians in there drinking, people of all ages, it was great. I thought: 'If only I could get something like this going in Milton Keynes.' I found that the stadium where we held Charity Music Day and I worked on the market has a really good, big bar and it's not used on a Wednesday night at all. I staged a 'one-off' night there and seventy people came so I'm going to try and make a go of it once a fort-night. I've wondered if it's the music that puts people off so I'm going to vary it from week to week.

Being out of work and having no money isn't easy, I should know, but some of these people who have been taken out of a rat infested squalor in London just turn their brand new Milton Keynes house into the same kind of dump they came from. They can't see further than the fact they've been given a bit of a break. I'm always having arguments with people about it. Perhaps the Corporation have provided plenty of sports facilities but what does that prove? They've built a wonderful up market shopping centre full of John Lewis' and Waitroses but its surrounded by forty five working class estates. I'd like to live in America. I still reckon it's the land of opportunity.

# The Artists' Tale

## GORDON FAULDS & ALEX LEADBEATER

*A new city needs people who are prepared to put down roots, but it also needs a transient population if it is not to become stagnant.*

*Gordon and Alex make no excuses for the fact that, for them, Milton Keynes is a stepping stone. Meanwhile it affords them a lifestyle in which everything is geared to their artistic careers. The sacrifice they make is in the sheer hard work which is necessary to maintain their independence.*

**Gordon:** After we left Art College we opened a group studio in Lancaster for up to seven artists, called 'Start studios'. Then we worked as handyman and housekeeper for an estate agent who had a large house outside Lancaster. It was quite dreadful and after a year we decided to leave. Alex had a show at the Serpentine Gallery in 1981 and as a result was asked to show with the Anne Berthoud Gallery. Given that we wanted to be artists we felt that it would be advisable to move nearer London to be in closer contact. It wasn't a difficult decision as we had no social life in Lancaster. We selected several places within reach of London. The two main contenders were Bristol and Milton Keynes which we had come across on a Woman's Hour programme. I had also been particularly impressed by the sewage works when I'd driven past on the M1 and wanted to find out more about the place. We had seen the adverts on the Underground and at Euston and we were interested by the contemporary architecture. So we phoned up the Development Corporation who put us on to Paul Barry who was then due to become director of Linford Arts Centre and he gave us the favourable tour of Milton Keynes. He showed us all the best bits. Generally we were convinced by the optimism because the place was still developing, especially after the decay of the north. We knew that we couldn't afford to move straight into London and Milton Keynes looked promising.

**Alex:** The day we came to look round was a Thursday and I loved the market in the city centre.

**Gordon:** We got this house on Fishermead in April 1982 with very little trouble although we were offered one on Conniburrow . . .

**Alex:** but we turned it down because of the horrible imitation brick archway in the entrance hall.

**Gordon:** More because it didn't have a garage.

**Alex:** We were offered part-time teaching at the Arts Centre and started there in September with a Still-life drawing course.

**Gordon:** It was very early days at the Arts Centre and they were having all kinds of problems. The classes were very small, we only had about eight students and they were all interested in different things so it was very individual which was quite fun. They were all beginners — a large proportion were middle aged women who wanted to take up painting as a hobby so really they just wanted to know the basic foundations.

**Alex:** We put a load of junk on the floor and said 'This is very interesting to draw. Draw it!' They all shuddered at first and then gradually accepted it.

## A Logical Extension

**Gordon:** We enjoyed the experience of teaching but by the summer term we were only teaching one class of perhaps, three people. The Arts Centre was running into problems of its own by this time so we decided that if it was going to continue in this form we wanted to stop doing it. So we started the stall on the antiques market in Central MK which all tied in and was a logical extension of what we were already doing. We didn't like the clothes available from shops because they were poorly made and we didn't like the styles. So we tended to buy things from jumble sales and junk shops. We also furnished where we lived, throughout college and in Milton Keynes, with things that we came across from the same sources. Each activity is part of a whole concept. We began to process the items we acquired, separating them into different categories — things which we would sell straight away on the market to provide us with income, things for us to keep, like tables and

chairs or anything useful for our house and other articles that we would take into the studio and develop into works of art. Eventually we gave up the teaching and expanded the market stall. When we started the stall we relied on our own instincts and collected the sort of items we'd choose for ourselves. Obviously, things that didn't fit us or we didn't particularly like, we'd sell. But as you do it more you learn what people want to buy. From all the jumble we're confronted with we try and select items of particular quality — natural fibres like cotton, wool or silk — essentially because those items have lasted and will last.

## Doing A Service

**Alex**: It has to be said that we don't get that much from jumble sales nowadays. We might go to 12 jumble sales in a day and come back with three items that are any good. We mostly buy from people who bring things to the stall and we travel to other markets. We also know several people who are designing and making clothes which we'll sell for them on a commission basis. That works quite well.

**Gordon**: We see ourselves as doing a service. We're going out and doing all the hard work and anyone can come along to us and know that the items we've selected are likely to be what they want and are going to be up to a certain standard so there's some sort of guarantee in coming to buy from us.

**Alex**: Milton Keynes has a good market because it's right next to the shopping centre and people walk past and just come to browse. A real cross-section of people buy from us in Milton Keynes. We get middle-aged professional people buying suits and anybody who wants quality clothing but can't afford to buy it new. People are very complimentary about the stall and often comment about our display. Sometimes we get criticised by people who say 'I could've got this from a jumble sale' and we have to point out that they're paying for our hard work as well as our judgement.

**Alex**: It's very difficult doing the market and being an artist at the same time.

**Gordon**: At the moment time is so tight for us. Monday morning is generally used for administrative matters — debts usually! Then as soon as possible we try and get into our studios which are the other two bedrooms in our house. Generally we spend Tuesday in the studios as well. Wednesday is half and half, some of the time being spent pricing the stock and packing the van. We get up at 6 o'clock on Thursday morning to do Milton Keynes market. On Friday when we do Portobello we have to leave at 5 a.m. to get to London by 6, so we have to be out of bed by four in the morning. Portobello finishes at about lunch time so we might go and sort out any business like buying materials and travel home in the evening and if we're lucky there might be a Jumble sale or an Auction in the evening. Saturday we spend all day out buying, travelling all about the area and Sunday is pretty much a recovering day — we like to try and catch up on our sleep.

## Still Very Young

The next step for us is to get shop/workshop premises as the markets are taking up too much time and it seems like most of it is spent either packing or unpacking. We've chosen to get somewhere in London rather than Milton Keynes because we want to open the shop up to sell a combination of clothing and artwork. You can't sell paintings on a market stall but it would be quite acceptable to sell them in a shop. Also you can't survive as an artist selling in Britain alone and to sell internationally you really have to be in London.

**Alex**: Unless we find somewhere to both live and work, which is almost impossible we would continue to live in Milton Keynes.

**Gordon**: We only ever anticipated being in Milton Keynes for a couple of years so we've never really settled or gone out of our way to become 'members of the community'. We're more socially involved in London.

**Alex**: Most of our socialising here revolves around going to other peoples houses for drinks or a meal.

**Gordon**: I like spontaneity in my social life. I don't like formally organising things and this place definitely lacks potential instant nights out. All these things will come in time, the city is still very young, it's a case of being here to see it. I'd love to come back in ten or fifteen years to see how it's developed.

"Sometimes we get criticised by people who say: 'I could've got this from a jumble sale'. We have to point out that they're paying for our hard work as well as our judgement."

# The Punks' Tale

## DAVE & ALISON BANCROFT

*Their punk wedding made the national Sunday papers. Then they did the most outrageous thing of all — settled down and had a baby. Dave and Alison are living proof that you can't judge a book by looking at the cover.*

**Alison**: Me and Dave met at a band practice at Peartree Bridge. I was in a band called Ethnic Minority and Dave turned up and we've been together ever since that night. He was living at his sister's house in Tinkers Bridge.

**Dave**: That's right, because my sister was renting a house there. She was buying a house in Wolverton with her boyfriend so I persuaded her to let me and a mate take it over, paying the rent in her name. It was great but it all fell to bits and we ended up getting evicted. The next door neighbour reported us to the Development Corporation as my sister wasn't living there anymore. We asked if we could keep the house but they wouldn't let us, so we ended up squatting it. The next door neighbour was a bit strange. He used to play classical music really loud at about eight o'clock on a Sunday morning. Once he came round and threatened to break Jamie's bass over his head but we used to annoy him as well — Public Image with the speakers in the cupboards up against the wall and we borrowed Fictitious' P.A., for a while and played records through that. It was great fun — the summer of 1980. Anyway we'd stopped paying the rent and the electric had been cut off and eventually they came round to evict us, but we managed to stall them for a couple of days, bought a car and moved to Devon. Me, Alison and Jamie — and Tiggles came as well for the crack. My other sister had a council house in Devon so we went to stay with her. That was brilliant. We put disguises on. We dressed up as hippies because I had leopard skin hair and Alison had this huge mohican and there was no chance of getting a house in Devon looking like that.

**Alison**: I put a headscarf on and wore a long dress.

## I Dyed My Hair

**Dave**: And I dyed my hair black and borrowed winkle-picker boots and these really tight jeans and ended up looking like a bloody Spaniard. No wonder we never got a house — a Spaniard and a hippy! We moved back because we couldn't get anywhere to live and my sister was getting a bit pissed off with us in her house.

**Alison**: So we came back but still didn't have anywhere to live. Dave's Dad was in America at the time so we stayed in his flat. I hadn't even met the bloke and one day he just came back to find we'd moved into his bedroom! So we moved into his front room on the floor.

**Dave**: It's quite a little flat too.

**Alison**: So how we came to get married was because we kept going to the council to explain the situation. Dave's Dad was so nice to us and wouldn't take any rent or food money but we had to pretend to the council that he was really horrible and about to kick us out so they'd find us somewhere to live. The woman at the council was really nasty to us and said that she didn't know why we were bothering her as we weren't even married. I was so upset that I just said that we might as well get bloody married then. We started thinking about it and it began to seem a great idea. We'd get somewhere to live, loads of presents and we could have a party. Nobody believed us until we actually did it. The wedding day was really good fun. It didn't seem like I was getting married really, more of an event that everyone would be at.

*Dave plays the mad scientist with his Open University chemistry set. "It's just to broaden your outlook on life."*

Dave: It was in Bletchley Register Office and they said that no more than fourteen people were allowed in but it ended up with sixty people in that little room. It was great, people drinking beer and smoking joints in the Register Office.

Alison: I wore an army overall with all bondage straps and studs on it and I had my mohican and Dave wore bondage trousers. On the car we had black ribbons and we were supposed to have a black wedding cake but the lady couldn't make it because she was ill.

Dave: It was in all the papers, Sunday Mirror and everything.

Alison: I told the reporters not to put anything stupid but they did as usual.

Dave: They put a little photo of my Grandad with us in the paper. But they wrote about how he was wearing 'what is known in old-wave circles as a tie'. And they put pathetic headlines like 'Punk Love'.

Alison: We had a party afterwards at Peartrée and Fictitious played. It was a good night but we still didn't have a house.

Dave: It was five months after we got married that we got the flat. We made sure that we either phoned up or made an appearance at the council offices everyday. There wasn't much point because they always told us the same thing but it's good to keep on at them. They eventually used to say: "Ah, Mr. Bancroft," when I went in. If you already live round here it's so hard.

Alison: Fern was born last February. A lot of people assume she was an accident but she wasn't.

When I first told people I was pregnant they'd say: "Have you thought of getting rid of it?" Charming! No, it was quite upsetting at the time.

Dave: We lived in the flat for two years and Fern was born right at the end of that time. We'd been hassling for ages to get a house but it still took until two months after Fern was born to get one. We had letters from the health visitor because they said we shouldn't live in that flat with a baby. The back bedroom was full of Alison's brother's stuff because he was in the army and had been evicted from his flat. Anyway, we only had one bedroom effectively and sooner or later Fern was going to need a room of her own. All the walls were mouldy and it was generally horrible. The point is we notified them two months after Alison got pregnant and it took all that time for them to give us a house. They offered us one on Waterside which we went to have a look at. We got in because all the downstairs windows were smashed. All the kitchen units had been nicked, there was glass all over the floor and something had crapped in the kitchen. There were glue bags everywhere.

Alison: We went back and they said: "Oh, of course we'd fix it up." "Bloody right you would!" I said, but it wasn't on because they knew we'd got a kid. Then we asked for one in the crescent at Fishermead but they said in so many words that they didn't want people like us living there as it's a bit of a showpiece. But when we said we'd have one on Conniburrow we got one in a matter of days because it's three storeys high and nobody wants to live there.

Dave: I'm doing an Open University degree which I applied for when I was on the dole because I

knew they'd pay for it and I've been doing it for a couple of months now. After each course you complete you get a credit and six credits entitle you to a degree. But those six credits can be in any subjects. At the moment I'm doing a Science Foundation course which was what I fancied the most but I might change and go on to do something else. It's just to broaden your outlook on life.

Alison: People say we're modern-day hippies and that's really what the punk movement has become. There was a lot of anarchist activity in the sixties, it's not that different.

Dave: Again, it's down to image. The main thing that goes against people is a violent image and I don't think that applies to punk anymore. Most punk bands sing anti-war songs.

Alison: We're totally non-violent. We've never had a fight in our lives. If there's any trouble your best defence is always your legs.

# The Welfare Rights Worker's Tale

**YVONNE BROWNFIELD POPE**

*Bright, bubbly, enjoys a laugh — that's Yvonne. She has a serious side, though, which expresses itself politically through her work on behalf of the unemployed in Milton Keynes. Her concern is based on personal experience. The moral of this tale is that by helping others we can often help ourselves.*

I was unemployed in a new town knowing very few people, and I suppose the thing that started me off as a real resident of Milton Keynes was when I helped to start a residents' association. I got to know the local Labour Councillors through that and was quite impressed by them. I've been a member of the Labour Party since I was fourteen and was secretary of the Young Socialists in London. They'd just started up a Labour Party branch in the area and I went along. There were only ten or twelve people there but within eighteen months we had a membership of over one hundred. So I was kept pretty busy that year building up the branch — I was membership secretary.

Through the Labour Party I met various other unemployed people. They had a lot of problems because they'd moved away from where their families were. They were completely on their own. Very often they'd moved here with firms who had been given generous financial incentives to move to Milton Keynes. In some cases, after a comparatively short time firms were offered even more incentives to move somewhere else and so they'd close their factory down.

The majority of companies who come here bring workers with them because there's plenty of housing available. When new firms were expected whole streets were left empty, waiting for them to come. But when firms moved on they left the people behind. They'd settled here and put their children into schools. They weren't able to move on.

The big incentive in M.K. as far as firms were concerned was that there were no organised unions and that people would accept much lower wages. Milton Keynes was sold on that level. There is no history of industry here, where wages have been negotiated by organised unions. Small firms with few staff have been encouraged. Even the large firms who take up a huge area, in fact employ very few people because they are really computerised warehouses. They might employ just clerical staff and a few drivers perhaps. There's no big industry here. The only big areas were things like Wolverton Works which has been wound down a lot over the years. There is no tradition of, say, manufacturing industry, so there's no structure for organising decent working conditions or wages.

We decided to try and start something to help the unemployed and publicise their plight. So we started the Unemployed Workers' Union. We had a lot of hostility particularly from the T.U.C. who didn't at that time agree with unemployed people getting organised. They said that they should stay in their unions. But a lot of people didn't have that opportunity once they'd left their job — like me. We worked very hard, picketing dole queues and so on and got quite a few members. We wanted premises where unemployed people could meet and talk and get help and advice particularly regarding benefits. We managed to get some workers via a government employment scheme and some premises in Bletchley and started the Unemployed Workers' Centre. We had cases of unfair dismissal, unfair selection for redundancy and lots of problems regarding Supplementary Benefit which I deal with a lot now, working for the Welfare Rights Group.

Welfare Rights did a surgery once a week at the centre. They were so busy because of the rise in unemployment, so they took on two more part time workers to help out. I was asked if I wanted to apply, which I did and got the job.

Welfare Rights is an independent organisation concerned with all welfare benefits. After all we are supposed to be living in a welfare state.

*"I don't like the City Centre. You can't go in there at any old time, it's strictly for shopping. It was built on common land and it's no longer common property."*

We deal with everything from pensions to maternity benefits. We now produce a set of leaflets on how to claim benefits — from Supplementary Benefit to disablement pensions. Plus we talk to a lot of school leavers and so get involved with the government's Youth Training Scheme, of which there are many in this area. We inform school leavers of their rights on leaving school. Often they're still given careers talks in school with the assumption that they're all going to get jobs. But of course, as we know, more than half of them don't get jobs.

Unemployment in young people is a big problem because they're going to have such a peculiar attitude to work. They come out of school with hope and ambition and find there's nothing for them to do. At best they get a very low paid job. I know cases of young people working thirty five hours for twenty or twenty-five pounds a week. Or they get put on a scheme which is very often exploitation. The amount of accidents among young people working on these schemes is much higher than the national average for working adults. They have a low expectation of wages and when they leave the scheme and get offered a job at thirty pounds per week they think they're doing well. What really concerns me is that in a few years these people are going to want to get married and have a family and there is no way they'll be able to afford to. We're going to see a whole generation of very disillusioned young people, who at best are going to become very cynical and at worst are going to be very disturbed and have an unpleasant view of those of us who do have jobs and homes.

I think the idea of Milton Keynes was a very good one. Where we lived in London there was no way we could afford to buy a house. Also just the amount of people in London put us off.

Where we were living it was very crowded and we wanted to go somewhere a bit more rural. At first I felt a bit resentful because I thought of myself as a Londoner and didn't want to move away just because I couldn't afford to live there. But having decided to make the move we made the best of it and that kind of enthusiasm seems general here. People have to make friends and get out and about to make a life for themselves. Up until recently there has been no entertainment, nothing organised at all and anything we've done, we've had to do ourselves. But on the whole I like Milton Keynes. I wouldn't move away now. I like the area and the fact that it is new and that there are new ideas. Some haven't worked, and some, they should have known better, like the dreadful flat-roofed houses. They've been building slate roofs in this country for centuries, they should have realised why.

To begin with there was no culture as such. In any other city there would be a certain tradition even if it was only a museum. Here there was nothing like that but I think they have made the effort to bring in culture from the outside to redress the balance. It does make you feel less isolated if there are some cultural events going on. There's no theatre here. I think because there was no money to build a repertory theatre that they started this business of bringing in professional directors and producers to work with amateur groups and use the facilities in the schools and so on. And in fact I've found that that makes for a much more enjoyable, interesting evening when you go to your local school which has excellent facilities and there's a production put on to such a high standard but using local people and professionals.

I'm a school governor at Conniburrow Middle school and I certainly get the impression that the schools in M.K. are much better than in a lot of the rest of the country. The teachers who came here knew they were coming to a new place and I've found that they are much more flexible. Indeed the standards here are extremely high. Stantonbury is a case in point. People have been waiting for it to fall flat on its face but it has proved time and time again to be an absolute marvel. Even if you take it on the traditional values of their exam results it's been proved to be highly successful. I'm sure this is another reason why people didn't want to move when their firms did because their kids probably wouldn't get such a good education anywhere else.

I'm very concerned that there are no houses for rent being built now. If young people have to move away to find jobs and homes you get left with a place that's full of middle-aged and older people and that way the heart is ripped out of a city. I can't see a vast upsurge of jobs coming here in the near future. We need government intervention to create jobs. We should be aiming to cut working hours without cutting wages. A new attitude to work is emerging because when young people leave school they can't expect to find a job and work there until they retire.

Of course this is a national problem but it is highlighted very neatly in a place like Milton Keynes. People here suffer more because they don't have the old family structure to fall back on.

# The Disabled Person's Tale

## ROSE KIRK

*People have many reasons for starting a new life. Some, like Rose, have no choice. Confined to a wheelchair by crippling arthritis, she has fought back all the way. Today she is an extremely active campaigner for other disabled people in the city.*

I've lived in Milton Keynes for three years now although I've lived in the area for about thirty years so I'm quite familiar with it.

The reason I moved into Central Milton Keynes was that I was working for a voluntary organisation called D.I.A.L. (Disabled Information Advisory Link). People who had problems to do with being disabled could contact us and we had information at our fingertips which could help them. At this time a lot of parties came up from London with a view to moving here. We told them, yes this was a good place for the disabled and yes, we'd heard from a very good source that the shopping centre was going to be all on one level. This was before it was built of course.

We thought that we could start a wheelchair scheme so that disabled people could come and go as they liked. They could do their shopping and have a meal instead of being left sitting in the car while someone else did their shopping for them. The corporation people who were showing these parties round latched on to what we were saying and asked me if I'd like to approach the Shopping Management Company with my ideas, which I did. They had already thought about something like this themselves but weren't quite sure what to provide. When I approached them it renewed their interest. They asked me to go along and voice my views and advise them on what was needed. I had thought about getting some battery chairs as I'd already acquired one myself and found it an absolute boon. I thought if the shopping centre could acquire some themselves, as well as manually operated ones it would mean that those who could cope with a battery chair could be absolutely independent.

Being disabled you can only go on shopping sprees when someone is kind enough to take you and then you just buy the things you need. It could be weeks, months or even a year before you get out again. I've had experience of this because I was housebound for eighteen months without once setting foot over the doorstep. I was quite alone. Therefore the Shopping Management Company realised I did know a little bit about it. They were very very co-operative and immediately set the scheme in motion. All this was happening a good nine months before the shopping centre opened. I was working with them, going round the shops which were still only three-quarters finished, to make sure that nobody put a step in where it shouldn't be, and that the walkways were wide enough and tills were accessible. They were tremendously helpful. They wanted me to do as much as I could because, as you can imagine, they had their hands full anyway.

## A Tremendous Feat

When it was all decided what type of chairs we would have, the shop keepers and various organisations donated enough money to buy twelve battery chairs — which was a tremendous feat. The Shopping Management themselves funded at least three of them and provided the office, telephone and storage space. They also approached me about three days before the shopping centre was due to open — which came as quite a surprise — to ask if I would consider running the whole thing. I had expected to volunteer to help two or three days a week perhaps, but I never expected that I'd be pushed in at the deep end on day one. I was a little bit nervous having been confined to the house for so long. It was a terrific strain but a beautiful one. At last something really worthwhile had been achieved. It was then that the Shopping Management suggested that I get a flat near the City Centre —

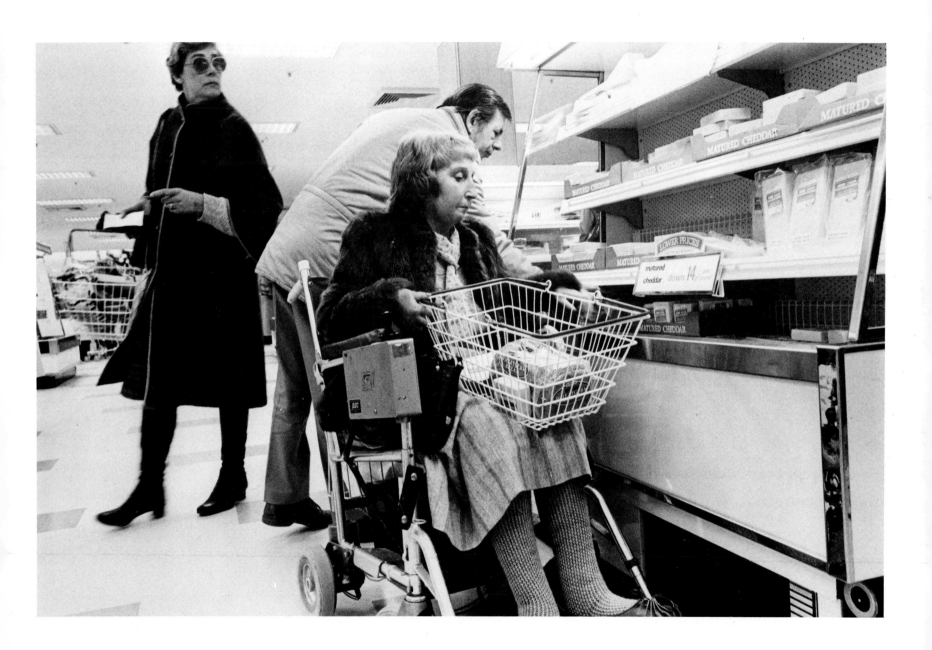

I was living in Stony Stratford — so I could be completely independent to come and go as I pleased. And if I felt I needed to go home for a few hours rest I could. So that was how I came to be actually in the centre, in the hub of things.

I resigned as organiser approximately a year ago because I had to have further operations and I was going abroad to see my son. I knew I'd have to have quite a bit of time off, so I thought it was only fair that I should put it on the line to them and then they staffed the scheme themselves. I still go in regularly to see how they're getting on.

I think the Development Corporation has thought quite hard about the needs of disabled people in the city. There's still more to be done but then this is a very new venture. They want to be told by the disabled themselves what their needs are. Milton Keynes Council for the Disabled liaises very closely with the Development Corporation and the Borough. They have a very strong Access Committee of which I am chairlady. We push for access to all public buildings. At the moment there is no law to ensure this, only stipulations or suggestions given to the architect. We hope within the next five years — definitely within the next ten — that it will be the norm, as it is in Scandinavian countries, for all buildings to be accessible to everybody. I think that the city is a good leader for the rest of the country. There are so many people looking to Milton Keynes for ideas.

Even so, there are buildings here that do not cater for the disabled — for instance the leisure centres (apart from Woughton Campus which is the most recent one to be built). In Bletchley one can't just go there, one has to phone up the management. They are very helpful. They help you get into the lift, which is great, but it isn't as it should be. We should be able to just go and use the lift by ourselves. Also the theatre at Stantonbury only allows two or three disabled people to go in there at any one time. Again, you have to phone up the manager and he will take you round the back because of the stairs. If it's raining you get drenched and it's a real hassle. So you think, 'Oh, I don't think I'll bother'. Do you see?

# Bad Access Points

I am on several committees to do with disabilities. I made a film for the Open University showing up bad access points, and also one about the pitfalls of trying to get a job. We are trying to encourage people who are building offices and factories to think all about this. We say to them things like: "What if your managing director had a bad accident tomorrow. He's a good man and he knows how to run this place from A-Z. He can't come into work anymore as he can't get in. It's only his legs that have gone not his mind. He's got a wheelchair but how does he come back to work? You will have to alter your building to accommodate to the costs of thousands of pounds, whereas if you'd provided lifts and ramps in the first place . . .?" Who knows, you go to bed all right tonight, but you don't know how you're going to wake up tomorrow morning and that's how these awful things happen.

I worked nearly all my married life. We were hoteliers. We worked very hard, a sixteen hour day for many years. I have two children who are grown up, and I did say that when they went I would stop working so hard and would think about doing voluntary work. Unfortunately my husband died. I'd had arthritis for twenty years and I'd worked all the way through it, fighting it, but on the death of my husband, with all the fretting and all the upset, probably my legs just folded up on me. I required many replacement joints so that was why I was housebound for all that time. It was towards the end of that time, when I was going to have a new hip, that the D.I.A.L. voluntary office started up and anyone interested was asked to get in touch. So I rang up the day before my ops. After the ops. I had about a week's convalescence, and within two weeks I was working in the office doing two afternoons a week. I became very interested in rights for the disabled and that led to everything I have now.

When I heard about the new city being built I felt like a lot of other people. I thought: 'Oh dear, what's coming.' Not many people liked the idea of their country lanes being stripped and new houses being put up. But when I was aksed to go round the shopping centre, which not many of the public had had the opportunity to do, I was quite amazed. My first trip round there left me completely speechless. I had no idea, I had never visualised the beautiful architecture and the beautiful floors, the big wide-open shops, words failed me. And that was only when it was three-quarters built. It's just fantastic.

As for Milton Keynes, my hope for the future is to see more in the way of entertainment for young people because so many young people move here, and soon enough their children will be grown up. If there's nothing for them to do they'll move away again. It's important to relax as well as work.

*County Fair, Milton Keynes Bowl, 1983.*

# The Refugee's Tale

**DAN VUONG**

*In 1979, when the Vietnamese government decided to expel residents of Chinese origin, Dan Vuong and his family were among those who made an arduous escape in a small boat to Hong Kong. A former biology teacher, Dan now works for the Elfrida Rathbone Voluntary Projects Programme. Through his job he is involved in helping other Vietnamese families start a new life in Milton Keynes. But he is also concerned that their children do not grow up ignorant of their past.*

My Father and Mother had a house and a business in Vietnam. But after the country became Communist everything belonged to the government and we had to leave with nothing except small things which were easy to sell. We used the money to pay the boat owner to take us out of Vietnam. It was a sailing boat made of wood, about twenty-five metres long. There were over one hundred and fifty people on board. We were on the boat for two months. There was nowhere to sleep, unless you could sleep sitting down or standing up. We ran into a big storm off the coast of China, it was very dangerous, very frightening. But all the time we were thinking: "We've got a new life . . ."

## The Important Thing Is Freedom

Eventually we arrived in Hong Kong, where we lived for nearly two years. During this time we were looking for the country we'd like to go to — we thought about America or Canada or England. I chose England because I think here there's more peace, more freedom, and life is not very hard. But the important thing is freedom. I think in America there is freedom but that also means freedom to carry a gun. And then there was the war . . . So I chose England.

I've been in Milton Keynes just over two years. When I first came to England I lived in a Vietnamese refugee camp near Chichester. The refugees who came to England all lived in camps at first, where they were taught English. I was there for seven or eight months, then the resettlement office asked me where I wanted to go. I had no homeland, no home even, but my sister was already living in Milton Keynes, so I decided to come here. It's a new city and I liked the idea of starting a new life here.

My first job in Milton Keynes was with the Christian Foundation in Wolverton, working on a Community Programme scheme. My English wasn't good enough for me to get a teaching job, so I started off as a building worker. I worked there for a year, and gradually my English improved. Then I got a job with the Rathbone VPP. Basically I'm a community worker and an important part of my job is acting as a link between the Vietnamese people in Milton Keynes. There are about thirty Vietnamese families here, about two hundred people altogether. Most of them have no jobs and quite a lot of them can't speak English. If they have to go to the health centre or if they have a social problem or money problems from the DHSS, or are looking for a job, I have to go along as interpreter.

On Sunday afternoons at Inter-Action I help run a Chinese language class, teaching Chinese children. They come to England and find the language quite easy to pick up, but they forget their own language. Some parents can't speak English so the children speak Chinese at home but they don't know how to read it and write it. We have three teachers and the children also learn drawing and painting and how to make things.

I have a wife and two boys, one thirteen, one eleven. They speak English quite well — much better than me. We all came over together from Vietnam. My younger son can't speak Chinese, he's forgotten his own language. After a few years here I think many Vietnamese children will forget their own story and forget where they came from. I don't think that's a good thing. They must remember why they came here. Some of my friends and I, we have the idea of one day writing

*"One day I hope there will be a real Vietnamese/Chinese community here, then we shall celebrate the Chinese New Year every year."*

67

the story about why we left Vietnam. We'll try to collect pictures of the day we left and the weeks we lived on the boat. I think it will be good for the children, when they grow up, to read about it and know where they came from. We hope that as a result they'll try hard in their new life.

As you probably know, Chinese people celebrate the new year differently than in England. All over the country, families get together for a celebration and hope for a peaceful and lucky year. In this celebration the dancing dragon is very important. The idea of the dragon is to wake up the Spring and bring luck for the year. Last year, for the first time, we held Chinese new year celebrations in Milton Keynes. So we made a dragon, some friends and I, to use in the parade. We have also used it on a number of occasions to teach the children how the dragon dances. One day I hope there will be a real Vietnamese/Chinese community here, then we shall celebrate the Chinese new year every year.

# The Shopkeeper's Tale

**NAYAB HAIDERS**

*Nayab and his wife Bushra were both born in Pakistan, though they met in Saudi Arabia where Nayab worked as an accountant for two years after qualifying at Newcastle Upon Tyne. Due to the instability of the Middle East he decided to come back to Britain, and they lived briefly in London before moving to Milton Keynes. Nayab found a good job with a locally based firm of accountants. He also helps Bushra run the corner shop on the estate where they live.*

In 1980 we were living in London, in Islington. The housing wasn't very good. You couldn't park your car outside your house, you had to have a resident's permit. There was no open space at all and it was so expensive to live. Going to work was terrible, getting squashed into the tube, and the transport costs of getting to work were very high. After four months we couldn't take it any longer. We wanted to move out of London but we didn't

## Ah That Is The Place To Go

want to go too far. We'd heard about Milton Keynes in the national newspapers and T.V. commercials and when I saw the advert for the job here I thought: "Ah, that is the place to go." I would say that Milton Keynes was much better than we expected. We moved into Conniburrow and couldn't believe it was a council house because it was such good quality. We were used to seeing council houses in London that are dilapidated and run-down. We were quite excited by it all.

I'm a chartered accountant with Peat, Marwick, Mitchell and Company. The work involves audits, advising on tax, VAT and income tax returns. The opportunity for business came along when MKDC were offering shops on the different estates and we thought it would be a very good idea to get one because my wife could run it. She was looking for work anyway and that would be an ideal job for her. There were a number of different shop premises that MKDC had built and we contacted them about taking this shop in Bradwell Common. It was brand new. We negotiated the rent and the lease terms and out of a few candidates they selected us to run the place. I think they were impressed by the opening hours

we were proposing. But neither of us had any retailing experience, so I'd be interested to know why the Corporation selected us. The hours we open are completely up to us. It is specified that this is a general store i.e. groceries, meats, tobacco, and confectionery. We try to provide everything the local community needs, which includes the traditional things and on top of that we do video films, collection of pools, we are an agency for a dry-cleaning company, the same with shoe repairs. On an estate like this the corner shop plays a central role. We know everyone and are quite responsive to people's needs. We'll definitely look into any suggestions and see if we can provide the service, within the economic restraints, obviously. People don't rely on this particular shop, it's more for odds and ends because we are so close to the Shopping Building. Because of better choice, competitive prices and all that people do their main shopping up there.

Business is what we expected, nothing more than that, really. As an independent retailer you cannot compete with national multiples. If we could beat the prices, yes we could do very well but there's no way we can. There's plenty of demand for the goods we sell and I wish we could be more competitive, we try our best. The business is financially viable as long as we run it ourselves but if we started employing people it probably wouldn't be economically worthwhile. We've never been broken in to but the mesh is there in front of the windows as we are being cautious. The shop has large windows and they are very tempting. If the windows were smaller we wouldn't have bothered with the mesh. The whole of the shop-front is made of glass. I find it a very surprising design for a purpose-built shop.

I would like to live for the rest of my life in Milton Keynes. It is such a nice place. It's

*Private housing construction, Bradwell Common. Built from the inside outwards, note how the wallpaper is coming off already.*

modern and all the amenities are here. You see all sorts of people here too. What we do miss here are places to go for an evening out. If you want to go to the theatre you have to go to Northampton or Luton. We go out quite a lot but mostly we invite friends to the house or we visit them.

# A Very Friendly Place

Milton Keynes is a very friendly place but the only problem here is the constant movement of population. Especially being in the shop we notice. People move in and out, you never see people really settle in. That's a characteristic of Milton Keynes. I think most people move about within the city usually from a rented house into one which they are buying. But from what we hear thirty to forty per cent move right away from the city. You see some faces everyday and you get to know them, you chat and you pick up the local news, who's doing what. We have to be very careful to keep things to ourselves — we don't want to offend anybody. But because of this influx and outflux of people you don't really get the village atmosphere.

Having qualified in England it would be difficult to fit in to accountancy and tax practice back home. Legally there is no difference but in practice things are very different. I could have studied and qualified in Pakistan but I wanted to come to England because basically English qualifications are considered to be the best in the world. I'd like to go back to see the parents sometimes, and I miss my parents but really there are other considerations that come first. If I make my future come first, then homesickness must come second. There's a big distance between us but we write or telephone. But they can't do a lot to help us. If they were nearby they could look after the children sometimes. I wish we had our family and relations or even good friends who are sincere near us, people who could help us if we needed it.

My ambition is to have a very big business or possibly a factory of my own where I would be looking after the financial side and using my accounting and tax experience. I work for a very big company anyway and I'd rather work with my own company.

We are Moslems, but I wouldn't call myself a practising Moslem. However, we wouldn't do the things which are prohibited by Islam. We wouldn't drink alcohol or eat bacon, pork or ham. But having said that, we try to mix with the local community as much as we can — dress-wise and in our day to day living. We're sociable, I'll go out to the pub and drink orange juice. We are supposed to pray five times a day but we find that with my wife looking after the business, my job, and the children we find no time. We would like to pray and when we do we feel really satisfied. If we pray once a month I feel we've achieved something. There is no mosque in Milton Keynes or anywhere like that where we can go.

Our children are growing up and we would like them to grow up into good Moslems. But as we are not practising Moslems they will never know what it is to be a good Moslem or what the principles of Islam are. If there was somewhere you could send children to learn the way of life then we would want them to go. Or if there was, say, a teacher at their school who had special duties who could teach them what Islam is. It will be very hard for them to ever learn. It will never come into their lives at school and at home they don't really see anything about being a Moslem.

# The Volunteer's Tale

## TOM SAYERS

*Tom is a latter day Robin Hood, always ready to help a friend in need. In spite of a pretty hectic personal life, this human dynamo is involved in several charitable ventures locally. He specialises in practical solutions to other people's problems — and he succeeds by breaking all the rules.*

I was born in Dublin in 1943 and I'm married with six children. Coming to Milton Keynes was an accident. I was working in West Germany for the British Government laying television and telephone cables. I got the job because I can speak German and English and we were working with a German crew. It was a great job, simple and straightforward, and it involved a lot of travelling. But my wife hated Germany. We lived in a little village right on the North-Eastern border where British people are a definite no-no. It was one of Hitler's strongholds. In fact, one of the men in my work crew used to be a sergeant in the S.S. I read in an English newspaper that British Telecom were building a new telephone exchange in Milton Keynes. I'd never heard of the place. It could have been a village near Timbuktu. I said to my wife: "How would you like to live in England?" "I've never really thought about it," she said. The only time she'd been in England was when we'd passed through on the way from Ireland to Germany.

My boss arranged my transfer to the U.K. and we kissed Germany goodbye. We spent a day in Holland, got the ferry to Felixstowe and travelled to Milton Keynes. We went straight to the Development Corporation offices. They told us our house wasn't finished and we could either live in a caravan park at Ashland until it was ready or pick another house. We decided to stay in the caravan and have a look round.

What I didn't know at the time was that the anti-terrorist squad were looking for me. Half an hour after we'd left Germany a bomb had gone off in the telephone exchange where I'd been working. Two soldiers were killed and many people injured. A man who fitted my description, Irish accent and all, was seen leaving the building. A few days later our house at Gibbwin was finished and we moved in. After a while I got the idea that people were watching me but I couldn't explain why. I didn't know what was happening. I was in the house one night and all hell broke loose. Front door, back door — I'm sure if they'd had helicopters they would've come in through the roof as well. I was taken to the headquarters of the Thames Valley Police at Kidlington, quizzed and grilled. They checked with Scotland Yard. They checked with Dublin. I was the most wanted man on their list, but of course, I was in the clear and they let me go. That was how we landed in Milton Keynes — with a bang.

After all that hullabaloo I decided to look for another job because the money at British Telecom was so pathetic and it was shift work. I went to work for Llewellyns the building contractor where I became their maintenance plumber. I am a plumber by trade. But that didn't last and eventually I was made redundant.

I have a lot of energy and I need to burn it off in some way. I became involved with Channel 40, the local cable T.V. station. At that time Channel 40 were just finishing doing the television side of things and going over to radio. One of the first jobs I did was to build a radio studio and I sound-proofed another studio for them. I thought that I'd love to have a bash at doing a radio programme and they said: "No problem." I got a real kick out of doing that. Then, when the news was announced that Milton Keynes was going to have a hospital, a campaign started for a 'buy a bed' appeal. We decided to do a radio marathon. Different D.J.s were going to go on every four hours and we'd have competitions and people could pay to hear a particular record. At the last moment I had the crazy idea of doing the whole marathon myself without a break and get people to sponsor me. All my job

*A helping hand . . . Tom contemplates his next scheme over a pint at the Suffolk Punch.*

was supposed to be was to stay awake but I ended up doing the broadcasting as well. I did eighty-four hours of it and at the end I was completely wrecked. On my sponsorship alone, we raised £1570, and we bought five beds.

After that CRMK went downhill. The money was tight and neither the corporation nor the general public felt they were getting value for money. It was all on cable which meant that you had to plug your radio aerial into the T.V. socket in your house so you couldn't listen to it in your car or whatever. I got a bit disillusioned and started looking for another avenue to channel my energies into. One day, by chance I went to the Pilgrims Bottle on one of those boring nights when there's nothing to do except go to the pub, and I noticed the Linford Community Workshop building right opposite. I went in and had a look round and someone asked me if I wanted to do a bit of pottery. I said: "You must be joking, but I'll give you a hand if anything needs doing around the place." I went on the Users Committee and twelve months later became treasurer and the next year I was chairman.

I got to know Vikki Bennet who runs a refuge for battered women and their kids in Bletchley, I'd seen some of the problems that these women had to put up with and I decided that I'd like to give them a hand. So I devised a scheme where the Development Corporation — God bless their souls — would provide transport so I could take the kids out and give their mothers a bit of a break. I had to convince the Development Corporation that I was 'one of theirs' — which I wasn't. I'm still not. I got over that obstacle by getting to know some of the nicer directors in the Corporation. By now I was a trustee of Milton Keynes Community Workshops and I was given permission to drive the Corporation van assigned to them. But I really needed a mini-bus for the kids outing so the next step was to swap the van. I found out which departments had mini-buses and when they were available. That information came fairly easily. So then, usually every weekend, I'd take the van to Stacey Bushes, park it in the Corporation garage and exchange it for a mini-bus or a staff car, or the executive bus, depending on who I was taking out. I'd fill it up with Corporation petrol — Bless 'em — and take the kids out for the day.

Another group that I stumbled across was a home for the mentally handicapped in Bletchley. I was down at Coffee Hall workshop one day and saw them doing pottery and woodwork. I thought they were marvellous and then I found out that they were often stuck for transport to get them about. I went to see the people who run the home and said: "How would you like me to take a bunch of them out on a day-trip?" It was Christmas time and we took them off to Woburn Wildlife Kingdom. I went up to Stacey Bushes, got this big eighteen-seater Transit and we were off. It was the 28th December and of course everything in the Safari Park was closed. We asked them to open up the Dolphinarium. I said: "You've got to feed the dolphins sometime so why not put on the whole show for the kids." The man said: "You're mad. It's freezing, we've been using a bulldozer to clear the snow up here." We got stuck too, we had to get towed out by a tractor. It was fabulous, the kids never even felt the cold. We drove right round but it was so cold, most of the animals stayed indoors. Eventually the Development Corporation twigged the transport thing when the petrol bills started to come in. So they put the mockers on and for a while it made life a bit difficult.

Probably the biggest event in my life happened this year when my wife was pregnant, my daughter was pregnant, my sister was pregnant, and they were all due on the 27th March which is my birthday. My wife nearly came up trumps, she went to the 28th. Ten days later, Caroline, my daughter gave birth to a baby girl, and the day after that my sister also had a daughter. So in the space of a couple of weeks I became a dad, again, a grandad and an uncle.

I've been waiting twelve months to go into hospital for an investigative operation. I got a computerised letter the other day — Please report at Stony Stratford Health Centre on Wednesday morning. I went down there saying: "What's this? Am I going for my operation?" And the doctor says: "No, this is the vasectomy clinic!" I had asked my doctor in passing about having the chop but he said that there was a twelve month waiting list. Anyway, this doctor says: "Tell me your circumstances." And I told him: "Daddy, Grandad, Uncle . . ."
"How many?"
"Six"
"Holy Shit," he says, "you can go straight to the top of the list!" I came out of there laughing. The wrong clinic on the wrong day; it could only happen to me.

I definitely want to stay in Milton Keynes. At one stage I got a bit homesick and went back to Ireland, but once back there I thought: 'Christ, who wants to come home here?' You don't realise how much you take Milton Keynes for granted until you leave it. I think I'll spend the rest of my days here. I did own a little plot of land in Ireland that I was keeping for my retirement but I sold that about five years ago. I see myself staying here and maybe with a bit of luck I might just get a job here too.

74

Leisure: "The diet for Milton Keynes is far from stimulating." (Derek Walker)

# The Witch's Tale

## DOT HORSPOOL
## (MADAME MORGANA)

*They used to burn them at the stake. Even in these enlightened times they still provoke a lot of controversy. But if fire couldn't destroy their faith, what hope have words?*

*Dot is the White Witch of Milton Keynes. She follows the Path of Wicker, an ancient pagan way of life based on peace and love. Her house is a covenstead — which means that she is prepared to welcome people who need her help twenty-four hours a day.*

I arrived here long before Milton Keynes, twenty years ago, from Wembley and I've been working continually for the good of the community. My daily life consists of helping people, poor people — helping increase their self-esteem, sorting out their problems. Sometimes I just sit and listen to them, the night is a lonely time for people on their own. Sometimes they can't stand the stress of a new city, so they take to drink. So we show them they are lovely people and don't need to drink. We give them hope.

## Mondays Is Tarot

Mondays is tarot reading. I only do two people a night and take a lot of time to go into it in depth. Tuesdays is a closed class. I teach my neophytes — which means novices. I teach them my witchcraft. On Wednesdays we have an open evening. We start with an invocation. That's a simple prayer that says: "Let the plan of love and light and power and peace work out." We believe in the power of peace and love. Then we do healing, absent healing for the ones we love and care for, also people in other countries — Belfast, the Middle East — and the plants and animals. Then we have a subject. It could be anything, reflexology, astrology, scrine (crystal gazing) or tarot reading. There's a big cross-section of people who come to my house on a Wednesday. Sometimes as many as thirty people come to the classes. We finish with another prayer and have coffee and biscuits and a general chit-chat. Thursdays and Fridays is again tarot reading and at the weekends we travel the country doing various psychic festivals doing readings etc. So you can see we're always busy at Witchy-poo Mansion!

A lot of people hear of us through the radio, T.V. and lectures which we do quite a lot of — W.I.'s, Mothers Clubs, Young Wives, even Stantonbury Campus which caused a bit of a stir. People were worried because I was telling children about witchcraft. These were sixteen year old adults who knew their own minds. And let's face it, I'm not going to give spells or incantations to a campus of sixth-formers so they can turn their mothers into frogs or toads.

I used to do the horoscopes on the local radio and one day the gentleman who was interviewing me before I started my programme said: "Help us with the weather, Dot, it's been so horrible." So I said: "Right, everyone who's out there listening, get up and open your windows and put out a positive thought to make the sun shine." And I believe three-quarters of the people who were listening automatically got up in their homes and did this. And believe you me, for the next forty-eight hours we had beautiful sunshine.

I've watched the new city being built brick by brick. I've seen the rape of the countryside and I've seen animals re-build their burrows. The badgers have left their sets, and the common's gone in Bradwell. I can no longer walk in my beautiful Linford Wood because there is a road right through it.

There is a great unrest with the overspills from London. We have a mixed community here, there's poverty and breakups of marriages like it's going out of fashion. So people have to learn to find themselves. They can't cope with this modern environment. There's a need for witchcraft or Wicker. Once they learn about themselves they can cope with living in this big, new city.

Twenty years ago I lived in these old railway cottages and I love them. We're losing our heritage, the bulldozers and the J.C.B.'s are moving in everywhere. They ought to preserve the old buildings. My first husband was employed by British Rail in Wembley and lived there in a railway house. When they pulled my house down in Wembley, they said I'd have to go where they put me. Fate intervened and I ended up in Buckinghamshire. So with my six kids, the guards can plus a B.R. container with all my gear in, we arrived here twenty years ago. We had an outside toilet, cold water — I had to put an Ascot in — tin bath to scrub the kids. But we were happy and I liked the houses. What's been done now with the Rainbow Co-op could have been done then and all the houses would have been saved instead of having to live with that monstrosity across the road.
(Permayne)

# The Rainbow Coop

When they knew the new city was going to be built, British Rail in all their wisdom decided to sell off all the railway cottages to M.K.D.C. So as people moved on or died the houses became empty, boarded up and then just started falling down. I was put on the new estate up the road (St. Peters Way) and hated it. There was a bath, but it was so new and impersonal I was always waiting for: "Hi-di-hi, it's time to go home now!" When all the railway cottages were going to be pulled down I got involved with the Rainbow Co-op and we managed to save this one street, Spencer Street, which is now one of the best running housing co-ops in the country.

All the children come and see me and I'll take their loose teeth out for them and produce 10p's from behind their ears. In Summertime they bring me flowers and also the school is right next door, and the kids say: "The witch lives there." I knew a lot of their mums when they were children so I'm Nanny Dot to a lot of them. They knock on the door and boast to their little friends that they know the Witch, and of course I have to find a minute or two to spoil them.

A while ago we had some visitors staying in the Street. It was a Summer night and they'd been to the New Inn and had a few bevvies. Afterwards they were standing outside talking when suddenly these bats started winging down the road. One of the visitors looked up and said: "Hallo, Dottie's got her relatives staying."

# The Community Worker's Tale

**TRACY WALTERS**

*In social terms, Milton Keynes is the biggest transplant out in Britain to date. It's a city of severed relationships. Consequently, there is a need to stimulate the growth of new ones, to accelerate the natural processes of community development. But what a daunting task. And what difference can the work of one individual make? Tracy is a very down-to-earth sort of person. He isn't put off by the enormity of the problem — nor by the realisation that what he does is just "a drop in the ocean".*

I came to Milton Keynes nearly six years ago specifically to work at Inter-Action. I'd been looking for work around people. I wasn't sure if it would be youth work, community work, theatre or whatever. I followed several lines of enquiry that led me to Inter-Action. I was given three months work on the summer project and doing a bit around the grounds and I've been here ever since. Let me explain. Inter-Action is a youth and community centre, an arts centre and a city farm — that's the definition. It's a place where, within certain limits, people can come and do the things they like to do. That can vary from gardening, looking after horses, having a picnic, looking at animals or doing arts or radio projects. The idea is for people to fulfil themselves, to like themselves and hopefully to go out and make Milton Keynes a bit of a better place to live in. That's what we try to do anyway.

## We're Just People

I'm the Project Manager but I don't want to appear like the oily rag that's become the engine driver. It's difficult to put a definition on what I do. I've been around for a long time, I've done a lot of work, therefore I'm aware of the problems in running the place and it's just up to me to work alongside everyone else and use the knowledge I've gained to help the place run smoothly. Roger is the director but he's Roger, I'm Tracy and Lois is Lois. We're just people doing a job.

All manner of different people and groups use Inter-Action — Intermediate Treatment, schools, policemen, Vietnamese people, youth clubs, people who want to do workshops or just look at the animals. The main thing is, we give them a chance. We're not so interested in what they've done, as what their potential is. We try to show people their own worth but I realise that Inter-Action is just a drop in the ocean. People don't always like what we've got but there are plenty of other centres doing other things which might interest them more.

Most people don't even know where Inter-Action is but it would be greatly missed by all the people who have enjoyed the place. I've never been anywhere so long and it certainly wouldn't have held me if I hadn't thought it worthwhile. I've seen its ups and downs but through it all I still think it's a good joint.

I'm in a band called T-Bone-2 which used to be called the T-Bone Boogie Band which evolved from a jam band. All we're out for is a good time and to put on a good show. We work in pubs and do some charity work. We have even played at the Open University and the Stables but it's just really a knees up — Jazz, Rock and Roll and Rythm and Blues — but just so people can dance and have a laugh. There's no need for anything more than that.

I live in Spencer Street but I came in there through the back door too — that's not to say I skulk around corners — but Spencer Street was already set up and going before I came to Milton Keynes. Through my work I met Tina who I've now lived with over five years and Tina lived in Spencer Street. We began our little affair which developed and that's how I moved in. I think Spencer Street works well. The fact is, it's survived six years and that's the proof. It's a group of people trying to be a community and I think that they are. It's not bound together by any philosophy, but its strength for me is its diversity which does mean that sometimes the ideals aren't reached and tasks aren't completed. We don't get up at eight o'clock and bow East or eat sandals and knit our

*Tracy heads the T-Bone Boogie Band at Charity Music Day, 1983.*

80

own yoghurt, well, some people do but I'm more of a boots and beefburgers person! I don't think I'll live there for ever but to ask if I'd live anywhere else in Milton Keynes is a hard question.

I'm a very content person these days. I'm content with myself. I'm not smug, but I like being me. I like my job and my relationship and I like where I live. I'm not ambitious and I'm spoilt and I'm richer than most people in the world already. Many people don't eat and live in countries with heavy politics and I consider myself very fortunate. There are millions of things I want to do or develop but I'll do them in the fullness of time. But no, I'm not ambitious. Being realistic, I don't think human beings have got a lot going for them. That's not to talk about individuals. I like individuals, but I really think we're heading for destruction — not necessarily nuclear, it could be pollution or over-population or a million and one other things. But we just don't seem to get it worked out right. That's one point about Inter-Action: if people can come here and learn that they're special then they can lead a fuller life themselves. You don't have to be famous to be special, most people are much more talented than me. I've just got a lot of bull and that's what gets me through.

# The Workshop Manager's Tale

**SUE SENIOR**

*The community workshops in Milton Keynes were set up to provide city residents with the resources to 'do it themselves'. Between them, they are equipped for such diverse activities as woodwork, computer programming, pottery, welding, printing, textile crafts and photography. Sue's job is a demanding one, involving creative, technical and administrative skills. When she started she also had to cope with the pressure of being a woman in a man's world — and the prejudice that goes with it.*

The workshops are a direct product of Milton Keynes being a new city. When I came here there were only three workshops in Great Britain and they were all in M.K. The idea came from Cindy Hargate and the Corporation who thought there ought to be one on every housing estate. They stopped with three. In fact I don't think there should have been one on every estate because there wouldn't have been the time, the room and the resources. Sweden, for instance, had one in every town and there are some in Canada. There are others being set up in cities near us and they've been to see us about it. These three in Milton Keynes are the first of their kind — very revolutionary.

## Anyone Can Come In

The policy of this place is that we have an age range of nought to ninety, so we have a creche at one end and we work with geriatrics at the other — any shade, creed or colour — and that's written into the running of the workshop. We also have special sessions for the physically handicapped and the mentally ill — you name it.

We're basically here as an open resource centre. Anyone can come in at any time and use the facilities which they can't, in essence, afford to have in their own homes. If you're unwaged it costs twenty-five pence for three hours and there's something like fifty-six thousand pounds worth of capital equipment for that amount of money — it's very heavily subsidised. You can also get guidance and teaching.

The workshops are working and fulfilling their purpose but it's the same with the leisure centres, you've got to educate the public into using them. This is why we've got such a hot policy for children. You've got to start getting the kids in first and then the rest of the family.

I came to Milton Keynes because my husband was fed up with his job in Yorkshire and got a job at Cranfield doing wind technology. We got a council house through Cranfield and so I arrived as a housewife with a small baby in 1979.

The first I saw of M.K. was in the middle of the night from a layby. I was breast-feeding my son and he was covered in milk and that horrible packet baby food and it was snowing. I thought: 'What the hell am I doing here?" and from then on it got worse. We drove down from Yorkshire and moved in at midnight. Martin said: "Behind here is a hill with trees on." And I thought: "Yeh, I believe you." And in the morning I saw I was on an estate (Bradville), so my initial impressions were very confused. I wrote to Stantonbury Campus and got some evening class work there teaching pottery. I wanted to get back to work so much. I felt very isolated and spent a lot of time in the house or meeting the neighbours.

I couldn't find anywhere to go with a child. There weren't any creches and he was too young for playgroup. Anyway, I started teaching at Stantonbury and the kiln blew up and Ieuan Jones said: "Fire the pots at the Workshop." And I said: "Hold on, what's a workshop?" I was literally half a mile away from Linford and I'd never heard of it. I cycled over there and I couldn't believe what I saw. My degree was in graphics and here was all the litho equipment and stuff that I hadn't seen since I was in college.

About a month later I started a little firm on my own doing macrame kits and came down to Linford to do some printing for it and had a fantastic time. They said that they were looking for a manager for the pottery side. I phoned up Cindy Hargate and said: "I'm the woman you need." The Linford job didn't actually

*Coffee Hall community workshop.*

83

come up before the Coffee Hall job which I applied for and got.

Coffee Hall was in a terrible state when I started. There was no storage space and the place was full of dust. There were no users and the place was in debt. It was very run down and had a dreadful reputation. The workshop had attracted a certain kind of person which didn't include women or children or grannies, in fact none of the estate. It was basically men between the ages of twenty-five and thirty. They wanted the workshop as their club. The day I came to interview here they were welding a car with gas bottles which is illegal and incredibly dangerous. The car had a full tank of petrol, you know? There was a tremendous feeling of aggravation a) because I was a woman and b) because I wasn't going to have things as they were. I had to face a massive six months complaints procedure of them against me until they resigned and went.

# A Really Good Place For A Woman To Be

Milton Keynes is a really good place for a woman to be. It's one of the few places that employ women in management without feeling bad about it. It's got good child care — if you're prepared to pay for it. And it's so easy to move here. It is also easy to get things going because people are new and interested in new ideas. If you give them a sheet of A4 saying this is what I want to do, nearly always it's acceptable or possible. They're with you, with the growing spirit which is just not true in other places I've worked. You know, usually everybody immediately gives fifteen reasons why you can't move the furniture. Here it's so different. I've said that the workshops can spin on a sixpence, but after the Development Corporation is gone it'll probably be a lot more difficult. In a lot of ways it's a whizz-kid city.

In a physical sense the city is great, just a very different concept. Well, it's changing a bit; in the first stages when you came to the city you couldn't see anyone because we're all behind sort of hills and everything. My Father-in-law said, when he was planning to visit us: "Oh, I'll ask someone the way." And we said: "You won't you know, because you won't see anyone." That was very foreign to him. But that's the good news. It's great on the estates, knowing your children aren't going to get run over. Fifty-one per cent of Fishermead was under five years old when I first came here. My son Eddie never has to cross a main road and my ex-husband (now) was telling a colleague in London that Milton Keynes is the only city where he could get out of his city house and cycle through two parks and in ten minutes he would be in his very high-tech office, you know, and next to a lake. It's a lovely city to live in.

I've been here nearly four years and I'm very aware of the fact that although I've learnt a great deal and we've got good things going here, I don't have any dance, theatre or cinema. These are the areas I feel I need to develop in and I can't do in this building. So I want to leave, I also want to move continents. There's always time to move on and I want to leave all this to someone young who can grow through this as I have. I'll never leave this place in my mind — it's been such a colossal part of my life. This is very much a young person's job and I honestly think you should boot people out after five years. You need somebody with all-energy and all-input. I want to run a bigger workshop with better facilities in another country. And if I've got to move I may as well get warm too. It was an accident of birth that I'm in Britain. I love M.K. and if it was by the sea you'd never get me out of it. I also object to have a cruise missile fifty miles from my back door, so I've decided that the Southern hemisphere is definitely the place to be.

# The Headmaster's Tale

## TREVOR JEAVONS

*As headmaster of a special school, Trevor has special responsibilities for the children in his care. It's a kind of job which could easily take over his whole life — if he let it. Because of this, perhaps, he isn't exactly your typical head teacher. Self-confessed "lunatic pianist" in a rock'n'roll band, would-be sci-fi writer, his life is woven with many threads.*

Before I came to Milton Keynes I was working in Cambridgeshire for the Spastics Society at their biggest residential school. My wife spotted an advert which said that a headmaster was required at a day special school in Milton Keynes. The angle seemed to be that the school was to be a resource for the community. I wasn't particularly looking for a new job but this looked like it would be a new sort of job. Anyway, they must have been short of applicants because I got it. The building had been waiting empty and boarded up for a year. Either funds weren't available or things couldn't be made ready to start when the building had been finished. It was the difference and the challenge that brought me to Milton Keynes. All my family wanted to come which was lucky, they thought it looked an interesting place.

Oliver Wells School is a day school for children disadvantaged by physical or visual handicaps. We don't have dozens of kids in wheelchairs because a lot of the problems are hidden, asthma for instance. The main thing is that these children could not cope with ordinary school life. Hopefully, after a period of time at Oliver Wells they can move into an ordinary school situation but that doesn't always happen. If you've got a child of good intelligence but who cannot move or speak, it takes a lot of work and a lot of research to put special equipment that child's way, so that they can communicate. It sometimes turns out that they have to stay in a special school for a long time. The age range here is from two years old in the nursery right through to eighteen year olds and although there's no official provision for them when they leave, we do try and help them either find jobs or continue studying.

I'm not satisfied with the provisions made for disabled people in Milton Keynes. Some thought has gone into it, but it's the old story, unless you or your best friend have been stuck in a wheelchair you don't think about wheelchair access which is basically what we're talking about. For instance, at the railway station the only way onto the platform for a person in a wheelchair is using the goods lift. You're stuck in the baggage compartment anyway, because if you're disabled that's what you are when it comes to public transport. Things look alright until you're stuck in a wheelchair. The answer is easy, all you do is get all the councillors and architects to spend a day in a wheelchair and then the whole world changes.

## The Lunatic Pianist

My hobby is the T-Bone Boogie band. Some head-teachers play golf, some are in the local choir, I'm the lunatic pianist in a band. I suppose it is more extrovert than most. Actually, a lot of my teacher friends do amazing things but because I'm in T-Bone everybody knows about it. I don't know what people say behind my back — perhaps that I should be sitting at home reading about disability, I don't know. Generally I don't think people think you're better at your job if you only think about one thing. But to everybody in the band day-jobs come first because that's where our main interests lie.

I trained as a painter — an artist, not a painter and decorator, and one of my sons is at art school. I'd like to be a good artist — whatever that means. I'd like to study sculpture, I'd like to write. I did write a book called 'Art and Cerebral Palsy', and I found that interesting. And I wrote a long paper for the Spastics Society on severe subnormality and art. I've been to Iceland to lecture on art therapy and my wife and I have done workshops in art therapy in Portugal and

86

we're going to lecture in Athens this Autumn, and probably going to Dublin this Easter so that's a nice hobby too. That's an extra thing we do but unlike T-Bone people don't know about it. Art is an occupation anyone can do. If, magically there were forty-eight hours in every day, I wouldn't be T-Bone Boogie-ing all over the place I'd be into lots of other things. I'd like to write science fiction, I'd like to learn to play the guitar properly — and the piano. So I can never be contented. Life is usually very ordinary but we can make it extra-ordinary.

It might look to others as if the Jeavons push our children into things we're already interested in. My daughter Della is in a caring job, she's a psychiatric nurse, but we never got her the job or had anything to do with it. I have the feeling, certainly with my own children, that if you try to get them to do something they go and do the opposite. For instance my son Dylan plays bass and he once or twice played with T-Bone Boogie, but he doesn't want to at all because what I'm involved in is finished, it's dead, it's geriatric rhythm'n'blues and useless as far as youngsters are concerned — quite right too, that's a healthy attitude.

The only bad thing about Milton Keynes is the negative people. I'm surprised how few people do things or fight things here. I've seen this apathy in teenagers, old people and the disabled. Milton Keynes is a good place but you can't just sit and wait for things to happen, every-one has to do their own little bit for the community.

"It's easy to forget but at that time this country moved into the grip of a real depression."
(Dusty Rhodes)

# The Gay's Tale

**MARC MASON**

*A second-floor room in Netherfield, painted black. The ceiling is hung with ex-army camouflage netting. Apart from a double mattress on the floor, the only other furniture is a dressing table with a mirror, and a stool. On the walls are photographs of Marilyn Monroe and other cultural heroes: also lots of well-hung young men.*

*Marc is one of a new breed of pioneers pushing back the frontiers of convention.*

I'm twenty, born in Bedford, moved to Milton Keynes a year later. Went to Lord Grey School. I was a punk at the age of thirteen. There were a few other punks around but I was the best. I used to get in trouble for being lippy. I used to go around with all the girls at school and the boys didn't like it. They called me a poof and a queer but I didn't care. I used to wear black skin-tight trousers, string vests, kilts and a leather jacket with writing on. I had long spikey hair, loads of earrings and I was generally dirty — oh and a pair of steeltoecap boots. Can you imagine me in a pair of steelies?

## I Was A Punk

After I left school I got a job in a bakery making doughnuts. What was a laugh. I got on well with all the women. I was a really good doughnut maker and enjoyed the job until I moved out of my parent's house. I started getting into other things and couldn't get up for work in the mornings so I left.

I was a punk for a long time but I got bored with it and for two years I was a punk but didn't want to be one. Because I'm gay and was really young, sixteen-ish, I was sort of ashamed of myself in one way but not in another. I thought if I looked really hard and macho I'd be O.K. And then I met this bloke called Conrad who was a Futurist. I got talking with him and he told me that everyone knew I was gay so I shouldn't hide it. That's what changed me and since then I've just been myself. I was about seventeen and started wearing pedal-pushers and ballet shoes, frilly shirts, berets, scarves, fishnets — all futurist stuff.

I never really went to clubs then. I just stayed around Milton Keynes. There were loads of parties then and I only went around with Conrad and a few other people. We called ourselves the Six Masons because there were six of us who used to go everywhere together. We used to go to each other's houses and drink cider from the moment we got up to the time we went to bed and smoke dope all day, everyday. And we'd go to parties and do sulphate every single weekend.

Trevor was the next person to help me. I met him and he was gay and he was weird. I wasn't so weird then. We used to go to the Starting Gate and that's where I got off with him. I didn't know much. After then there was always competition between me and Trevor. We slagged each other down left, right and centre but we still liked each other. There was me and my crowd and him and his, the Braidy Bunch — people who worked in Braids Hairdressers. It was these two groups, always in the Starting Gate, all girls and gay blokes. Sunday night was funk night. Eddie Richards was the DJ and we got him interested in playing Futurist music and Gay Disco. But in the end we had to leave the Starting Gate as basically it was just a pub for 'grebos' during the week. The brewery had the idea of turning it into a disco pub as Sunday nights were doing so well. They promised us all sorts of things and Eddie thought we'd stay there for ever but they turned it into Austens. They got the wrong end of the stick completely. Austens is just a normal night club, they didn't understand what we were trying to do. I wasn't that involved then. I just used to go every week and get drunk.

The people and the music moved to Centrecom where there was no bar. You had to take your own drink in — usually we got it from the Starting Gate anyway! Then it moved to the Gladiators Rugby Club then Mr. J's in Bletchley. For a year and a half there was talk of moving to

*Marc at The Joint. It was never a drag . . .*

90

Peartree Bridge and then finally we did last year. Eddie asked me if I'd like to be more involved so I decorated the place. We decided to give it a name and call it The Joint. The name came about because of smoking a joint and because it was a real joint venture and in America the joint is a place of entertainment. We rushed to get it open. We painted everything black and draped black plastic everywhere and had loads of mannequin dolls. We advertised it and had Tik and Tok on the first night. Eddie booked all the bands.

# The Joint

The Joint has become a place where almost anyone can go, enjoy themselves, go over the top. It's just good fun I think. To me it's a place that's black, extremely dark, the music's brilliant, the atmosphere's brilliant, you can get drunk and do exactly what you want and have a really good time. It's more of a community thing than a club. All the bands that come and play, from London of wherever think The Joint is a brilliant place. Alien Sex Fiend loved it and said so in Zig Zag magazine. They reckoned it was their best ever gig. I'm in charge of how the place looks. When we first started it took ages to get ready every week because it's a youth centre the rest of the time. I used to get there about midday, get out by seven o'clock and have an hour to get changed and do my make-up. It takes about seven hours to do with four of us helping. It has to come down afterwards but I don't do that as usually I'm too drunk! But that only takes an hour as everything is ripped down. I usually go on the door until everyone comes in. I set an example. Does that sound bad? I sit at the door and try to put across what The Joint's about. I'm meant to be selective but I'm not

at all. Skinheads have been banned but I don't really mind that. They always look violent and we try to stop the children and the wallies from coming in. If it was up to Eddie it would be much more selective because then the club looks better and encourages better people to come. I never turn anyone away really. I don't like restrictions.

I'd like to be really famous but I'm just too lazy. One night after The Joint had finished me, Trevor and a few others — we were all really drunk — went absolutely mad, talking like women and chatting up all the men and being really over the top. We were so good we thought we should start a drag act. So I phoned up Trevor and Twiggy and they agreed to do it. This was two weeks before the Christmas Party and we decided to do it then. We borrowed the costumes from friends and bought wigs, we came on as nuns in suspenders with fire and bells to the music from The Omen and then we went into miming Maria off The Sound of Music album, then the Lonely Goatherd. We did Andrews Sisters records and the Shangri-La's Leader of the Pack — that one was my idea — and the finale was Divine and It's Raining Men by the Weather Girls. At the end

# I'd Like To Be Famous

everyone got wet and sprayed with shaving foam. We intended to do the show again but you see what I mean about being lazy? I'd like to be famous for everything I do because I keep changing my mind and my image and I kind of like the way I am. I'd just like to be famous for being myself. Whatever I did would be really good. I don't really care what happens to me as long as I'm happy and enjoying myself. I'd like more money but I can manage with what I get on the

dole. Everything else comes with money doesn't it.

What I hate about Milton Keynes is not knowing places to go. It's quite boring. I couldn't imagine not having somewhere like The Joint. I have to go out and do something every Friday night. I've lived here all my life and grown up with the place. I like the houses and the newness and all the trees here. I feel safe here. I wouldn't like to move to London as I don't know many people there and I'd have to go through it all again, getting to know people. I'd have to start at the bottom again. Ha!

# The Writer's Tale

## JACK TREVOR STORY

*Author of (inter alia) "The Trouble with Harry" and "Live Now, Pay Later", one-time Guardian columnist, TV personality — Jack really needs no introduction. So we'll just let him have the last word ..*

I came to Milton Keynes in January 1977 with an Arts Council Creative Writing Fellowship. My appointment was the first in this country. Usually writers in residence are attached to universities or colleges, mine was the first writer attached to a town. I was supposed to serve all the local schools and colleges and also look after the residents generally. What a year that was after zippy Hampstead with Liz Taylor and Dicky Burton living next door and Dud Moore popping in for moans. Here I was stuck in the mud or running around in my scruffy little banger like a mid-wife, delivering scrawled-over memoirs to little old ladies. The fellowship was officially for one year, but it is still going on unofficially after seven years, seven years and a bit. Last week the phone rang and it was another would-be historian: "I'm blind and my husband is dead and I want to write about him. He was a psychopath and used to show his genitals to children." I said: "Oh, yes." She said: "That is Mr. Story isn't it? Could you read what I've done and advise me?" I told her I couldn't. I said that my wife always insisted that I was a psychopath and I show my genitals to pretty doctors and anyhow I'm not interested in helping people to write books like that. Nor any books. Alan Edwards never gives up and Ricky Paris has been pushing short stories and novels under my nose for years. He's a very good writer but I can't get publishers and editors to even reply or return the postage. Writing today is an impossible business for beginners and also a distressed area for literature. My only outlet now is Radio 3.

During my official year I discovered what I could and couldn't do. I could not organise writers' workshops for instance, because I dislike them as time-wasting and depressing. Nobody can learn to write by going and mixing with dumb-clucks like themselves, reading their own rubbish to each other. They are not aiming at editors and publishers. They want the ignorant to applaud

## Oh That's Nice Gracy

them. Oh, that's nice, Gracy. Why don't you make it a bit longer? Amateurs have no idea what writing is. They think it's something they learnt to do at school.

I held some poetry readings but only because I was pressed. My wife said recently — she once worked for the Development Corporation — "The Corporation were very disappointed in you." They never tell you to your face but it wouldn't have mattered much anyway. David Crewe, press officer for M.K. about that time, once told me that my lousy television and radio and press pieces about this city had brought more publicity than the whole of his expensive department. I've met people since then — there's a black guy that works in the Post Office in the city centre and he said: "You made that terrible T.V. film about Milton Keynes, driving around the roundabouts and saying what a terrible place it is. We lived in London then but we laughed at that time and that's why we came here." The place sounds so ghastly that you simply have to try it. It's like emigrating to Australia.

I met Bill Billings. He's a good writer in the vernacular manner — also Robbie Burns was. The noo. Bill breaks all the rules. He's an anti-poet and I'm an anti-novelist. I love his attitude to poetry and prose and share it. Poetry buffs sit at readings and listen to John Silkin and Ted Hughes and are not allowed to clap until the end of the cycle, darling. I once cross-examined Silkin about this and he explained the reason, though I've forgotten it.

I've been here in Milton Keynes as I have said for about seven years, but I don't know anybody. If I go to a pub I take a book with me. There is nobody I want to have a drink with here. Having done all that I have done in the media, I have established the wrong kind of fame. The extent of communication is some stranger crying: "Hello Jack!" I cry: "Hello, um ah!" I know about a thousand um ahs. None of them knows who I am or what I do for a living. "What are you doing now, then?" Or "When are you coming on the box again?" They're all telly idiots and think television spells success for all those doomed heads they watch every night. Television is oblivion for performer and audience. Then you get the serious, thoughtful, intellectual, sober Milton Keynes people. They are much worse than thickoes and a bigger threat to the precious second of your day. With them you have to be a grown-up.

# A Marvellous Greek Temple

My *real* friends — Harpenden, Hampstead, Kent, London, half a dozen friends, eight kids — would never dream of boring your arse off with cultural conversation. With good people who last a lifetime you have crazy talk, girl crazy, boy crazy, sex crazy, but always cosmic, never specific. We live after all, not in Milton Keynes, but in the universe. I have never had a friend of even roughly my own age. My present wife is twenty-nine. Getting older, better look round. She was sixteen when we started living together in 1972.

In my television programme about Milton Keynes I talked to people like Fred Lloyd Roche. I like Fred, he's terribly formal and afraid of what you're going to write about him. I said:

"I think you've got quite a good city here. Well, it will be when it's finished and landscaped. What ruins it, surely, is all the scruffy people coming in. Don't you get fed up with all these bloody slum-types living in all your houses?"
"That's a very emotive thing to say." He replied, as though it was none of my business to say things like that. I said: "I went round the city centre (which I did) and thought it was a marvellous Greek temple full of dwarfs dragging their shopping baskets."

Trying to steady my mind for a last look, I think what we have here in M.K. is a very good piece of landscaping, now we need some houses to follow. There are no real houses, they're terrible places. Have you seen this new estate? Boxes with houses painted on them to make it look as if they've got wooden beams. They look like Elizabethan manors, but when you get close you can see it's all shit. It's all made of shit. My son came to visit, he saw these and said: "Whatever are they doing over there? Is that a film set?" I couldn't believe that, I said: "That's a place where people are going to live." And it's the same all over. If you go to that village, Little Woolstone I think it's called, it's a very good concept, they've made it look like an old English village but everything's too small. They've done what film people do, they've scaled everything down to save cost. They've cheated like they cheated Portmeirion, the village in 'The Prisoner'.

I find the shopping centre okay though I prefer Mr. Lavidge on East Road, Cambridge, who cycled our whole week's grocery on tick right out to Chesterton, like four miles. Waitrose will not do that. There are no pubs here — well, two. Most of them, like Milton Keynes shops and social services, are run by pushy charladies. "Wot chew 'having, luv?"

He's having one of his nasty turns.

I see the future here very much as other futures that are now past. I lived in Welwyn Garden City for about twenty years and many of my children and grandchildren still live there. I know Harlow and Letchworth, specially Letchworth, I know Peterlee and Washington. All have

# Eureka

improved with the years particularly those built in the thirties. Nothing to do with trees either. It's just that towns improve where the quality of the people improves. New cities and towns attract riff-raff and always get whoever happens to be dropping off the end of the nation's waiting lists. Welwyn used to be the badlands — the station caff was raided for drugs! — And now we are the badlands. One day the fugitives from the bailiff or the old bill will have left or died or grown a moustache and Milton Keynes will be like Welwyn Garden City.
Eureka.

*Private housing, Little Woolstone. "They've done what film people do, they've scaled everything down."*